The Crucifixion of Jesus in 30 AD

For Youth Groups, Jesus Lovers, Church Leaders, Bible Study Groups, and Families eager for a deeper understanding of our Lord Jesus Christ (Study Guide Included)

Debbie Dunn

FYI - Unless otherwise noted, most Biblical quotes come from either the King James Version (KJV) or the New International Version (NIV) of the Bible APP.

<u>Permissions</u>: This book or any portion thereof may not be reproduced or used in any manner without the publisher's express written permission except for using brief quotations in a book review. For copy permission, please email the author, Debbie Dunn, at moredunntales@yahoo.com. Place, in the subject line: **The Crucifixion of Jesus in 30 AD**

<u>Disclaimer</u>: The content used in this book is intended for educational and informational purposes only.

First Printing, 2024. Printed in the United States of America
ISBN: 9798227615473
Imprint: Independently published. Distributed by Draft 2 Digital.

T.R.E.A.T. Tales Presents

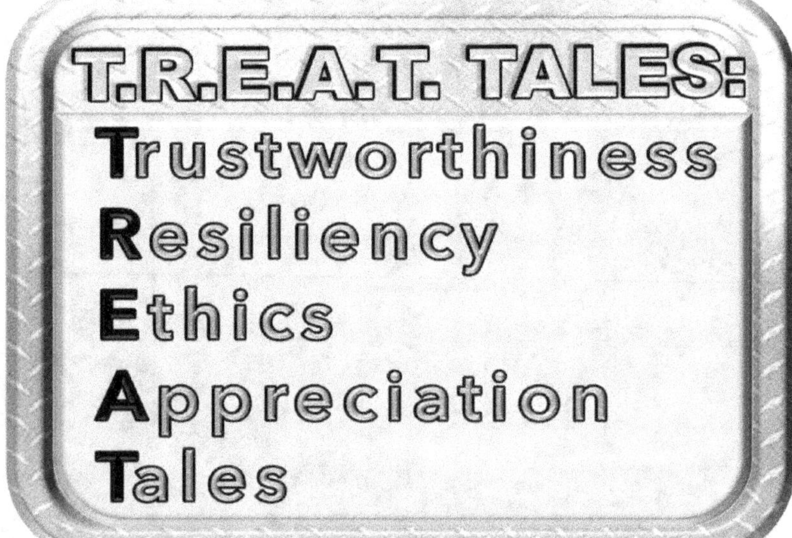

Website: https://bible-books-for-his-glory.com/index.html
Email: moredunntales@yahoo.com

About the Author: Debbie Dunn

Debbie Dunn has been a professional storyteller since 1989. She has also taught at-risk teens, served as an anti-bullying specialist, and taught elementary and middle school. In her retirement years, she indulges her love of our Lord Jesus Christ, nature, traveling, and writing as she pursues learning and exploring more about the Holy Bible.

The Crucifixion of Jesus in 30 AD is a book crafted explicitly for youth groups, Jesus lovers, church leaders, Bible study groups, and families eager for a deeper understanding of our Lord Jesus Christ. The author, understanding the unique needs of these groups, has filled this book with conceptual color illustrations that will resonate with them and has included a study guide for their convenience.

The main points covered in this book include:

- When Jesus kept dropping the Cross, the Roman soldiers found a man to help Him.
- Before the Roman soldiers nailed Jesus to the Cross, Before the Roman soldiers nailed Jesus to the Cross, He refused the vinegar drink to numb His pain.
- A '***King of the Jews***' sign was posted above Jesus' head.
- Jesus was mocked by the onlookers, Pharisees, Roman soldiers, and the two thieves nailed to crosses on either side of Him.
- Jesus did not speak during the three sunlit hours from 9 AM until noon nor when it was dark as night from noon until 3 PM.
- Discover the 20 types of Physical Stress and 8 kinds of Emotional Stress suffered in Jesus' final hours of life.
- At 3 PM, the 7 statements Jesus made from the Cross fulfilled some Old Testament Prophecies.
- **(1)** "**Father, Forgive them for they know not what they do.**"
- **(2)** When one of the thieves recognized His Holy Nature, he asked to be remembered when He came into His Kingdom. Jesus responded, "**Verily I say unto thee, today shalt thou be with me in Paradise.**"
- **(3)** From the Cross, Jesus spoke to His mother and Disciple John.
- **(4)** Needing a small amount of saliva to make His final 3 statements, Jesus said, "**I Thirst.**"
- **(5)** Jesus moaned, "**Father, why hast thou forsaken me?**"
- **(6)** "**Father, into Thy Hands I Commend My Spirit.**"
- **(7)** With His last breaths, He exclaimed, "**It is Finished!**"
- Jesus died on command a little after 3 PM on Friday of 30 AD.
- Jesus lovingly endured this excessive torture and death to atone for all sins committed by humans (past, present, and future). Won't you accept His free gift of salvation?

Fifty percent (50%) of all book sales will be donated to **Covenant House** to "***join the fight to end youth homelessness***."

FYI – This is a stand-alone book pulled from 25 sections of my 75-chapter book titled, "Jesus' Crucifixion and Resurrection foretold by 12 Biblical Prophets & Kings." Those 25 sections include:

The Crucifixion of Jesus in 30 AD	Jesus' Crucifixion and Resurrection … Book
Chapter 1 of this book is the same as	*Chapter 21 of my other book.*
Chapter 2 of this book is the same as	*Chapter 22 of my other book.*
Chapter 3 of this book is the same as	*Chapter 23 of my other book.*
Study Guide for Ch. 1-3 is the same as	*Study Guide for Ch. 21-23 of my other book.*
Chapter 4 of this book is the same as	*Chapter 24 of my other book*
Chapter 5 of this book is the same as	*Chapter 25 of my other book*
Chapter 6 of this book is the same as	*Chapter 26 of my other book*
Chapter 7 of this book is the same as	*Chapter 27 of my other book*
Chapter 8 of this book is the same as	*Chapter 28 of my other book*
Chapter 9 of this book is the same as	*Chapter 29 of my other book*
Chapter 10 of this book is the same as	*Chapter 30 of my other book*
Study Guide for Ch. 4-10 is the same as	*Study Guide for Ch. 24-30 of my other book.*
Chapter 11 of this book is the same as	*Chapter 31 of my other book.*
Study Guide for Ch. 11 is the same as	*Study Guide for Ch. 31 of my other book.*
Chapter 12 of this book is the same as	*Chapter 32 of my other book.*
Chapter 13 of this book is the same as	*Chapter 33 of my other book.*
Chapter 14 of this book is the same as	*Chapter 34 of my other book.*
Chapter 15 of this book is the same as	*Chapter 35 of my other book.*
Chapter 16 of this book is the same as	*Chapter 36 of my other book.*
Chapter 17 of this book is the same as	*Chapter 37 of my other book.*
Chapter 18 of this book is the same as	*Chapter 38 of my other book.*
Chapter 19 of this book is the same as	*Chapter 39 of my other book.*
Study Guide for Ch. 12-19 is the same as	*Study Guide for Ch. 32-39 of my other book.*
Chapter 20 is the same as	*Chapter 74 of my other book.*
Chapter 21 is a shortened Bibliography	*found in Chapter 75 of my other book.*

WHEN JESUS KEPT DROPPING CROSS, ROMANS FOUND A MAN TO HELP HIM

It appears that initially, the Romans tried to have Jesus carry the almost 165-pound Cross the 2000 feet from the Fortress of Antonia to Golgotha, which means *'The Place of the Skull.'*

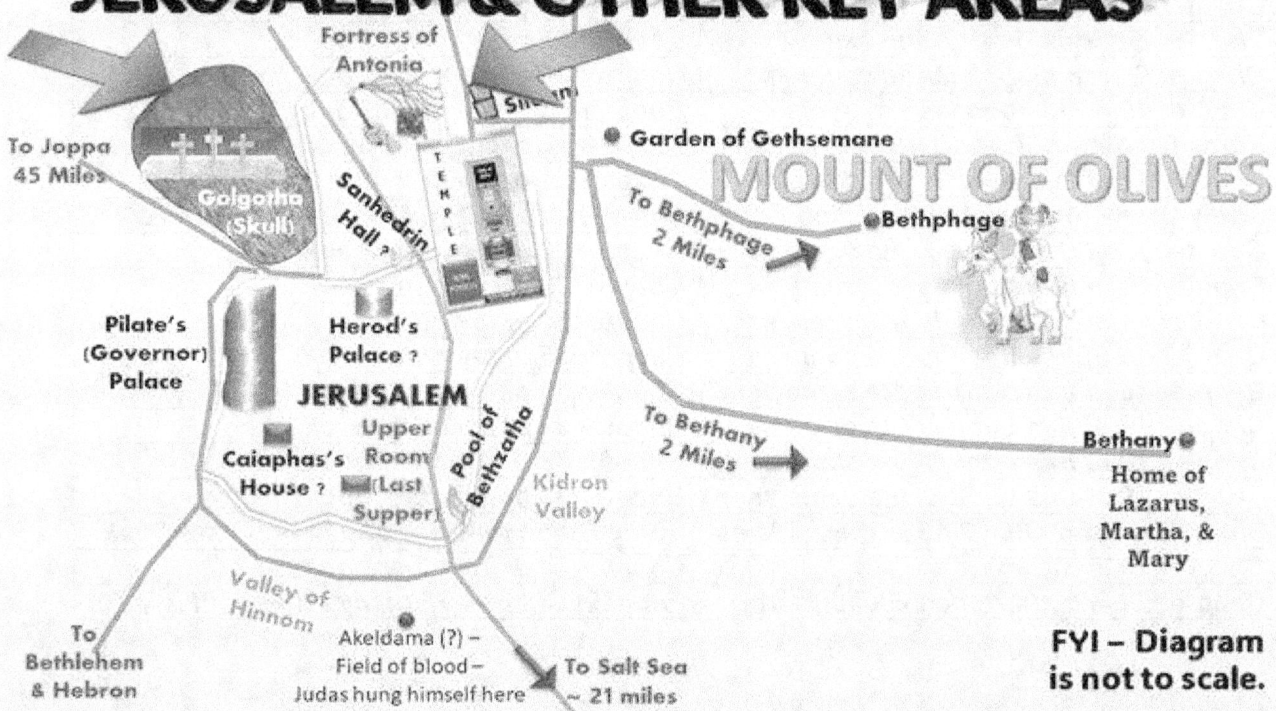

We learn in **Luke 23:27-31** that many people followed along with Jesus. A small group of women were wailing and lamenting for Jesus. Our Lord told the women they should redirect their feelings of angst from Him to the future of Jerusalem. The current year was approximately 30 AD. We know that the Romans destroyed the Jerusalem temple in 70 AD.

Examine 4 Gospels for Clues (KJV)

Matthew 27:32-33	Mark 15:21-22	Luke 23:26	John 19:17
32 And as they came out, they found **a man of Cyrene, Simon by name**: him they compelled to bear his cross. **33** And when they were come unto a place called Golgotha, that is to say, a place of a skull.	**21** And they compel one **Simon a Cyrenian**, who passed by, coming out of the country, the **father of Alexander and Rufus**, to bear his cross. **22** And they bring him unto the place Golgotha, which is, being interpreted, The place of a skull.	**26** And as they led him away, they laid hold upon one **Simon, a Cyrenian**, coming out of the country, and on him they laid the cross, that he might bear it after Jesus.	**17** And he bearing his cross went forth into a place called the place of a skull, which is called in the Hebrew Golgotha.

Likely due to lack of sleep, so much blood loss, dehydration, and bodily weakness, Jesus kept dropping this heavy Cross. Even if Jesus had been in good health and well-rested, it would have been quite challenging to drag a cross weighing about 165 pounds. The Roman soldiers noticed a large man named Simon from Cyrene. According to Mark 15:21, the man was the father of Alexander and Rufus. The Roman soldiers forced him to carry Jesus' cross.

There were likely many rewards in Heaven for Simon from Cyrene when he took his last breath. The Angels probably ushered him into Heaven with great respect and honors.

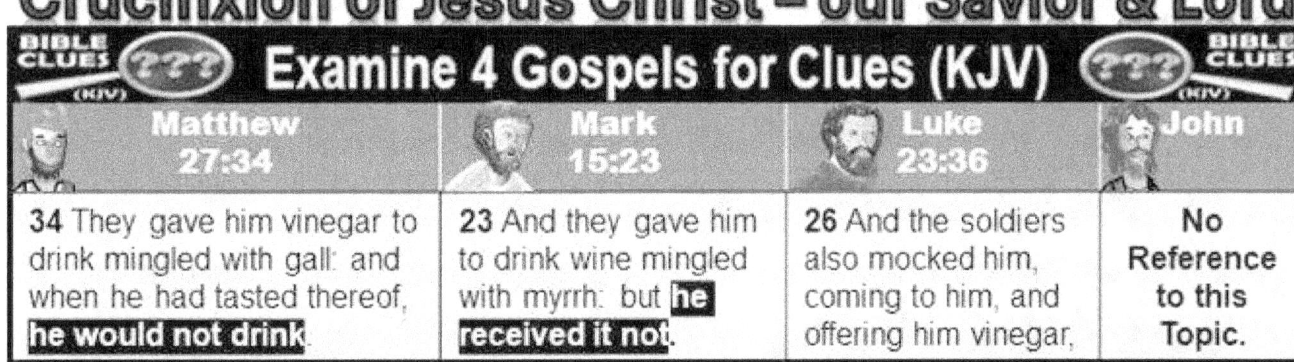

As stated below, Jesus did not allow Himself to be numbed from the pain by accepting the Roman soldier's customary drink offering of vinegar. He needed to keep His consciousness sharp to focus on the immense task of absorbing millions upon millions of our sins.

Crucifixion of Jesus Christ – our Savior & Lord

BIBLE CLUES (KJV) ??? Examine 4 Gospels for Clues (KJV) ??? BIBLE CLUES (KJV)			
Matthew 27:34	**Mark 15:23**	**Luke 23:36**	**John**
34 They gave him vinegar to drink mingled with gall: and when he had tasted thereof, **he would not drink**.	23 And they gave him to drink wine mingled with myrrh: but **he received it not**.	26 And the soldiers also mocked him, coming to him, and offering him vinegar,	**No Reference to this Topic.**

Psalm 69:20 Reproach hath broken my heart; and I am full of heaviness: and I looked for some to take pity, but there was none; and for comforters, but I found none. 21 They gave me also gall for my meat; and in my thirst they gave me vinegar to drink.

Deuteronomy 32:32 For their vine is of the vine of Sodom, and of the fields of Gomorrah: their grapes are grapes of gall, their clusters are bitter: 33 Their wine is the poison of dragons, and the cruel venom of asps. (KJV)

ROMAN SOLDIERS NAILED JESUS TO THE CROSS

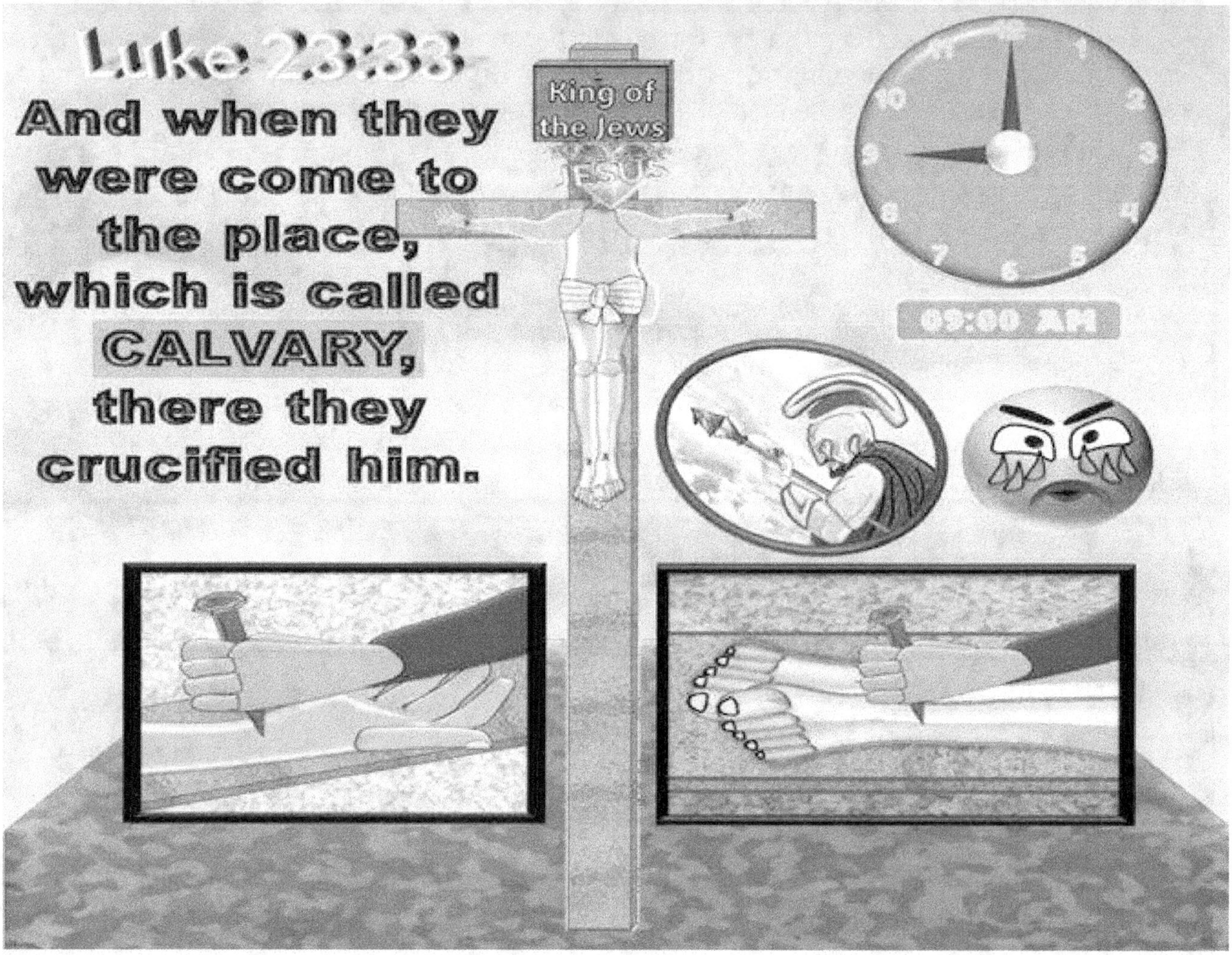

Luke 23:33

And when they were come to the place, which is called CALVARY, there they crucified him.

Crucifixion of Jesus Christ – our Savior & Lord

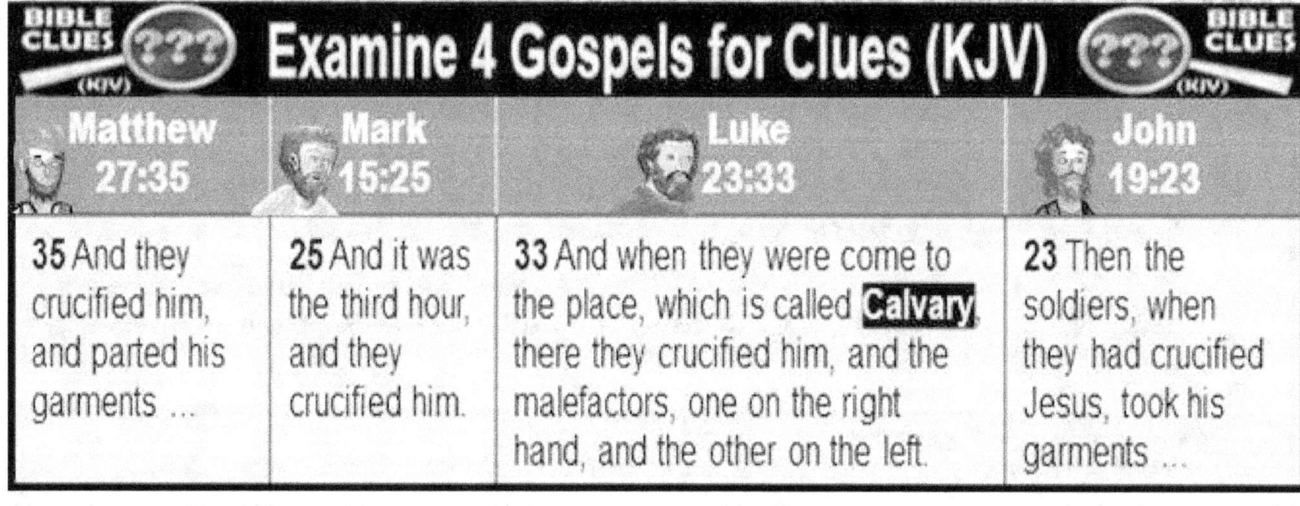

BIBLE CLUES ??? Examine 4 Gospels for Clues (KJV) ??? BIBLE CLUES			
Matthew 27:35	**Mark** 15:25	**Luke** 23:33	**John** 19:23
35 And they crucified him, and parted his garments …	**25** And it was the third hour, and they crucified him.	**33** And when they were come to the place, which is called Calvary, there they crucified him, and the malefactors, one on the right hand, and the other on the left.	**23** Then the soldiers, when they had crucified Jesus, took his garments …

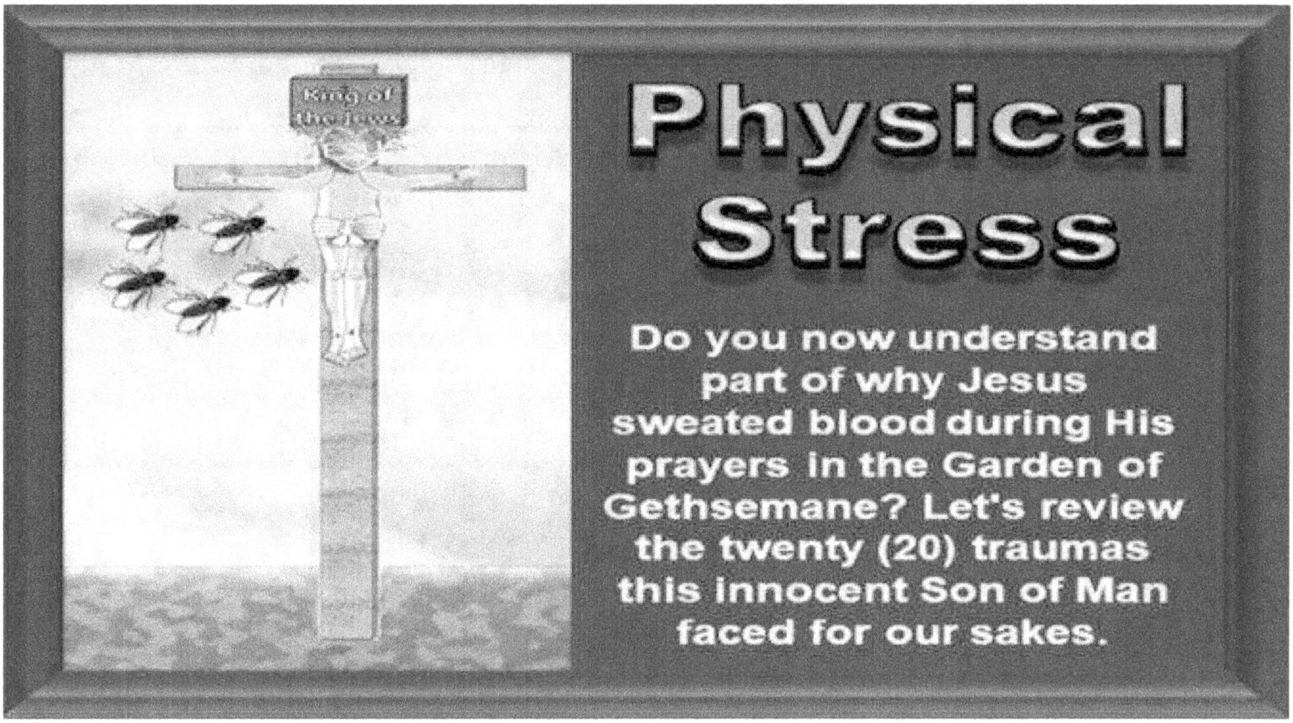

① Sweated Blood: Late Thursday evening, Jesus experienced so much fear and dread for the upcoming torture that He sweated blood during His 3rd prayer in the Garden of Gethsemane.

② Walked Excessively: After being awake all-day Thursday, the Sanhedrin arrested Jesus around midnight. Then, He had to walk from the Garden of Gethsemane to the house of Annas (about 1 AM on Friday) to the residence of Caiaphas (about 2 AM) to Sanhedrin Hall (between 3-4 AM) to Pilate's Palace (about 6 AM) to Herod's Court or Palace (about 7 AM) back to Pilate's Palace (about 8 AM). Before 9 AM, after receiving 39-40 lashes and a Crown of Thorns, Jesus had to try to drag Himself and the cross to the Golgotha site so the Roman soldiers could then crucify Jesus.

③ Sleep Deprived: As you can see, by the time Jesus was nailed to the cross about 9 AM on Friday, He had been awake for more than 24 hours.

④ Bled Internally: Due to whippings and being hung on cross, Jesus likely had bled internally.

⑤ Hands bound together: Jesus either had His hands tied in front of His body or behind His back from the time the Sanhedrin arrested Him and throughout His six trials.

John 18:12 **Then the band and the captain and officers of the Jews took Jesus, and bound him,** 13 **And led him away to Annas first; for he was father-in-law to Caiaphas, which was the high priest that same year.** (KJV)

6 <u>Slapped by Sanhedrin law officer</u>: When the officer attending the first of Jesus's six trials decided that Jesus answered Annas dismissively or disrespectfully, he slapped Jesus in the face.

> **John 18:22** And when he had thus spoken, one of the officers which stood by struck Jesus with the palm of his hand, saying, Answerest thou the high priest so?
>
> **John 18:23** Jesus answered him, If I have spoken evil, bear witness of the evil: but if well, why smitest thou me? (KJV)

7 <u>Deprived of food and drink</u>: Jesus was deprived of food and hydration. If that were true, the last time He would have eaten or drank would have been at the Last Supper.

8 <u>Beaten while blindfolded</u>: Some members of Sanhedrin blindfolded Jesus and did all manner of evil things to Him.

> **Matthew 26:67** Then did they spit in his face, and buffeted him (i.e., beat with a fist); and others smote him with the palms of their hands, 68 Saying, Prophesy unto us, thou Christ, Who is he that smote thee? (KJV) - Similar quote in Mark 14:65
>
> **Luke 22:63** And the men that held Jesus mocked him, and smote him. 64 And when they had blindfolded him, they struck him on the face, and asked him, saying, Prophesy, who is it that smote thee? 65 And many other things blasphemously spake they against him. (KJV)

9 <u>Mocked</u>: Herod and his men of war mocked Jesus.

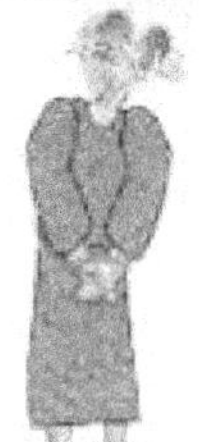

10 <u>Crown of Thorns</u>: The Roman soldiers shoved a crown of thorns onto Jesus' scalp. Then they spit on Him and beat Him about the head, embedding the thorns more deeply into his scalp.

11 Ripped Jesus' clothes on and off: Recall when you have had to remove a Band-Aid from your skin and how painful that was – especially if it yanked off some skin hairs. Now, imagine how the Roman soldiers ripped off Jesus' clothes three times. The first time was when they removed His clothes to place a Crown of Thorns on His head and a purple robe on His back. The second time was when they tied Him naked to the whipping post to scourge Him 39 to 40 times. The third time was when they removed Jesus' clothes to place Him on the Cross. The blood leaking out from the lacerations on His back, in various stages of clotting, would have ripped open again and caused excessive pain.

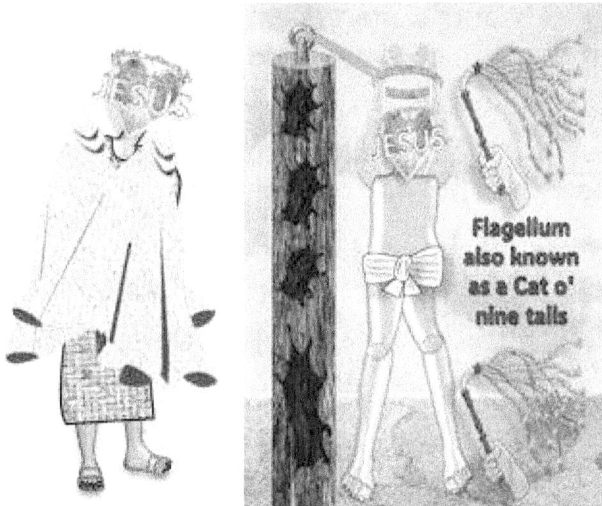

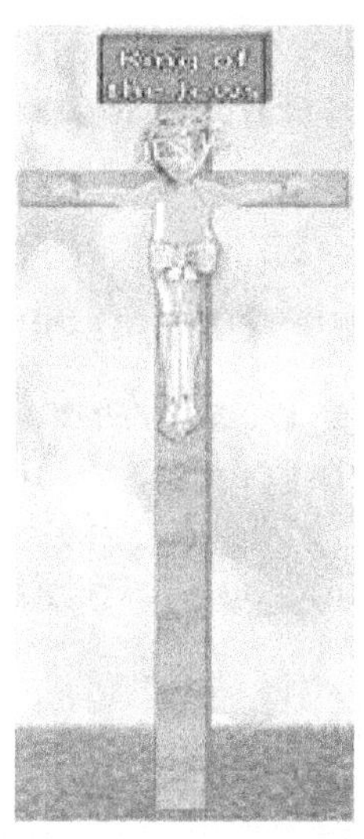

12 Forced Jesus to carry His Cross: The Roman soldiers forced Jesus to drag that cross that weighed about 165 pounds for a distance of about 2000 feet. They eventually had to grab a man from the crowd to carry it as Jesus kept dropping it as He fell to the ground. Even if He only had to carry the crossbar to which His wrists would be nailed, that alone weighed about 30 to 40 pounds. That wood, full of splinters, would have rubbed against His bleeding backside and His head.

13 Nailed Jesus' wrists and ankles to the Cross: The Roman soldiers nailed Jesus' wrists to the crossbar. They couldn't nail His palms as they would have ripped through and not held His weight. They also nailed Jesus' ankles to the main post of the cross. (FYI – I once broke my left ankle on both sides and shattered my right wrist from a simple fall. Due to the chemo treatments for my 2010 bout of breast cancer, my bones were brittle. The pain of that was beyond any pain I had ever experienced. I could not move my fingers, make a fist, or move or rotate my foot without the most unbearable pain. I had to have orthopedic surgery in both cases.) Just imagine that Jesus not only had to face the horror of having heavy spikes hammered into His wrists and ankles, but those same appendages would also have to hold up all His body weight. The suffering would have been absolutely excruciating!

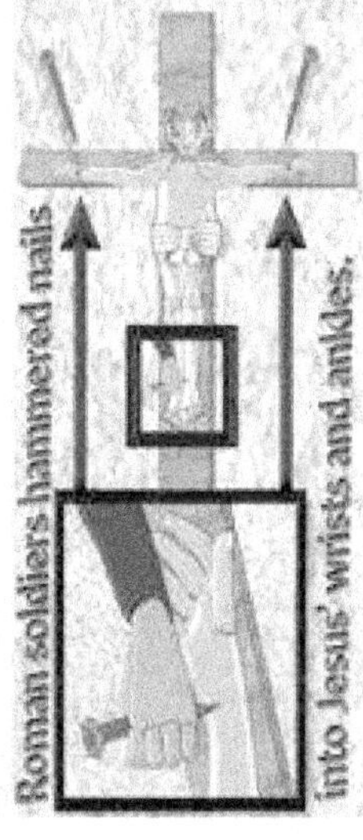

14 Dislocated Shoulders: When the Roman soldiers raised Jesus up on the Cross and allowed it to settle into the ground, this action would likely have dislocated both of Jesus' shoulders.

15 Dehydration: Jesus hung on the Cross from 9 AM until some point after 3 PM when He died. He had had no water since the Last Supper the previous evening.

16 Flies and bugs: Flies, bugs, and birds might have been attracted to Jesus' open wounds. Besides closing His eyes, He could not swat those insects away.

17 Itching: Have you ever had an annoying itch and suffered when you could not scratch it? Jesus had no way of doing that since the Roman soldiers nailed Him to the Cross.

18 Blood, Sweat, and Grit in Eyes: Jesus would have had blood and sweat dripping into His eyes and grit crusting His eyes. Jesus had no way of wiping this away.

19 Sunburned: Jesus' body would have been sunburned. Even though we always think of Jesus having His privates protected by a loin cloth, the Roman soldiers were bargaining for His clothes. So, that part of His body would also have been exposed to people's eyes and burnt by the sun.

20 Cramping and internal spasms: As Jesus had been tortured and He was actively dying, our Lord would have suffered extreme cramping and internal spasms.

Jesus did all of this for us!!!

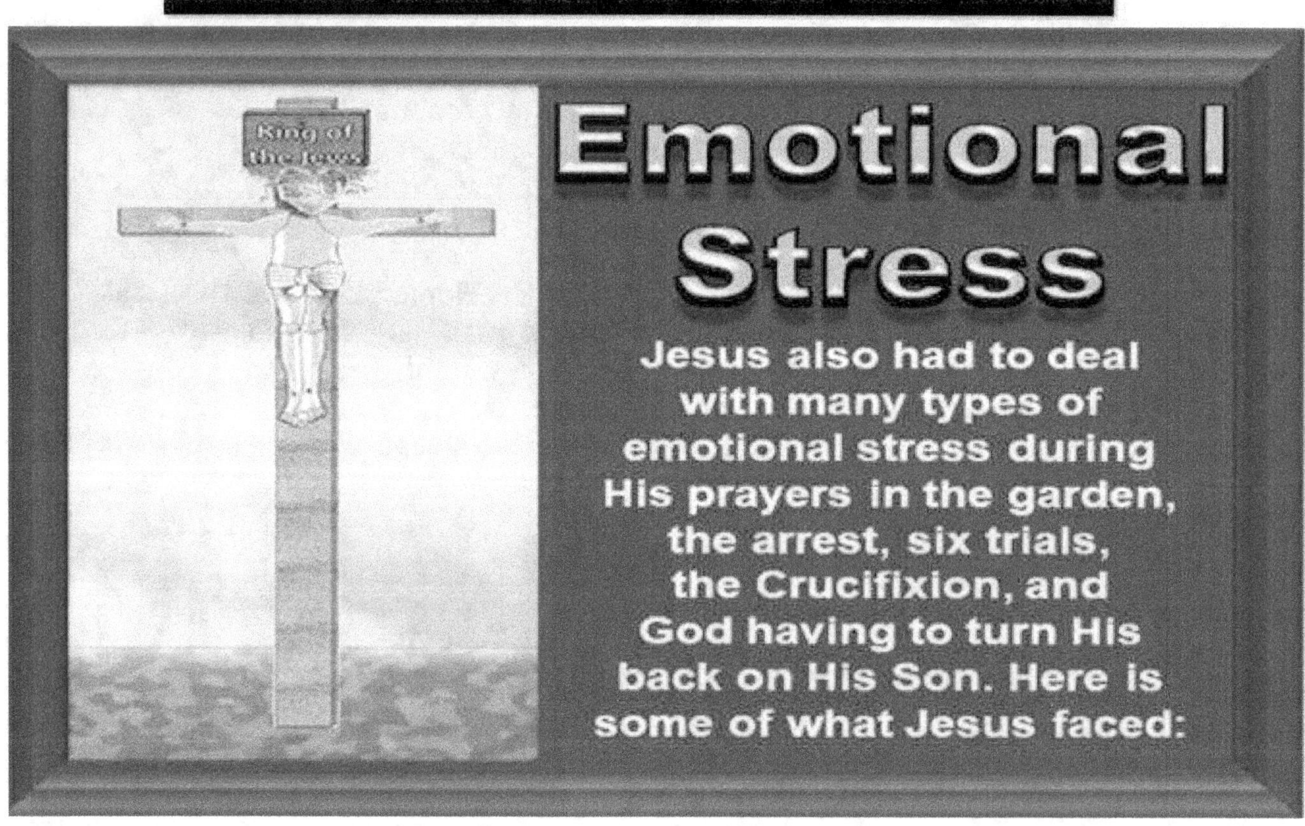

① Betrayal: Judas, one of Jesus' twelve Disciples, betrayed Jesus to the Sanhedrin for 30 pieces of silver. In the Garden of Gethsemane, Judas kissed Jesus's cheek. This kiss was Judas' way to identify the correct man for the Sanhedrin soldiers to arrest.

② Disowned by friend: Peter, one of Jesus' most trusted Disciples, denied knowing Jesus three times. Peter disowned Jesus within a few hours after declaring that this was an act he would never commit.

③ Deserted by Disciples: Except for Peter and John, the other nine Disciples scattered and ran away. Only John risked standing near the Cross with the mother of Jesus and some other women followers.

④ So fearful of upcoming pain that Jesus sweated blood: During Jesus' third prayer in the Garden of Gethsemane, He sweated blood. Thankfully, an Angel came down from the Third Heaven to comfort and counsel Him.

⑤ Hysterical Crying: In the Garden of Gethsemane, Jesus was so fearful of upcoming pain and separation from His Father that He was crying and wailing loudly.

⑥ Abandoned by God His Father: For the first time in thousands upon thousands of years, Jesus' own Heavenly Father felt forced to turn His back on His only begotten Son. Up to being nailed to the Cross, Jesus had never known one moment of separation from His beloved Father and the Holy Spirit.

⑦ This sinless man voluntarily became SIN for the sake of all humankind: Jesus voluntarily, by His Father's will, had agreed to become SIN. This sinless man was stepping up to the plate and allowing His whole being to absorb every single sin, large and small, ever committed by humankind: Past, current, and future human beings, even beyond 2024, when this book was published.

If you have ever committed any of those sins, then **Jesus died to save YOU**. In other words, we have ALL sinned. He died to save us ALL!

⑧ Can you picture how guilty Jesus would feel as He experienced the moments when each of us sinned or missed the mark?: It would have been pure agony. That is likely part of why He did not talk for the first six hours He hung on the Cross. He had to focus on living those sinful moments from our respective pasts, present, and future. These are just a few examples of what Jesus had to absorb. Jesus would feel:

☹ the indifferent cruelty of the Sanhedrin organizing His death and torturing him plus the atrocities committed by the Roman soldiers.

☹ the guilt of murderers and serial killers

☹ the proud defiance of terrorists such as what happened on 9/11/2001

☹ the arrogant pride of members of the Ku Klux Klan and other racists causing harm & devastation and sometimes murder of people of color

☹ the empty soul of those who feel no empathy or compassion such as what Hitler ordered and the Nazis complied with during the Holocaust

☹ the shame of sexual deviance of rapists, priests who sexually take advantage of children and teens, producers and agents forcing their clients to give into and providing sexual favors, sex traffickers, teen and grown-up date-rape

☹ the cruelty of bullies who try to get their victims to suffer unspeakably and sometimes kill themselves

☹ the callous, entitled indifference of those who commit identity theft in order to rob people of their money by hacking into their computer or phone or database

☹ the sociopathic manipulations of kidnappers

☹ the righteous and sadistic satisfaction of the inquisitors during the Middle Ages Inquisition

☹ the dangerous prattling of today's Influencers preaching that Jesus was never crucified or that God is dead or that their listeners should cause anarchy or commit crimes or trauma of various types

☹ ETC. ETC. ETC.

You might say, "Well, I never sinned like that. I'm not so bad!"

But every one of us is a sinner. We all have missed the mark at least once. If you have ever committed any of the sins listed on the previous two pages, you would be destined for wrath and an eternity in hell.

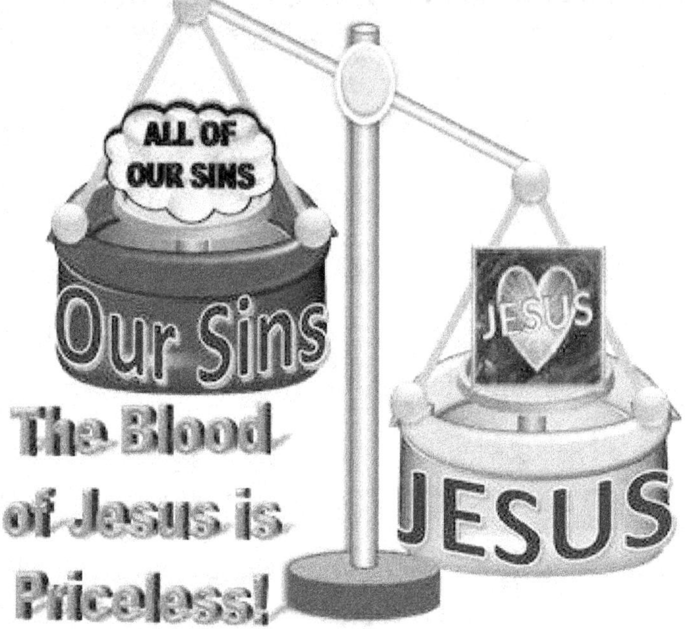

Jesus humbled Himself as a Servant.

Whether our sins were small, medium-sized, or oversized, we were destined to die for those sins and be sent to hell. The Triune God Agape Loved us so much that they decided to allow Jesus to live approximately a 33-year human life (perhaps a year or two longer) so He could become the sacrificial lamb who would be slaughtered in our place. Jesus stepped off His Divine Throne at the right hand of Almighty God, left His riches and Heavenly existence behind, and stepped into the trenches with us on earth. He humbled Himself to be a servant to us instead of our master. Examples of that included:

He washed the Disciple's feet at the Last Supper.

He actively worked on healing people. 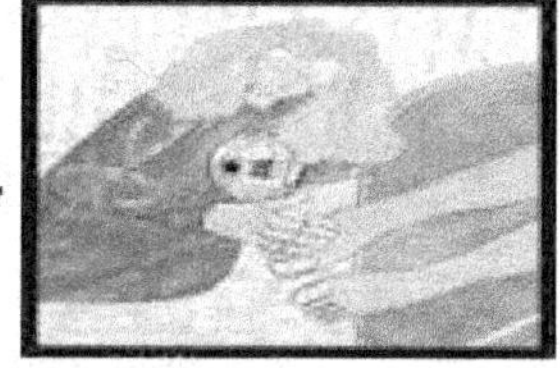

He turned water into wine at the Cana wedding in Galilee at the behest of His mother.

He fed the 5000-starving people in the crowd. 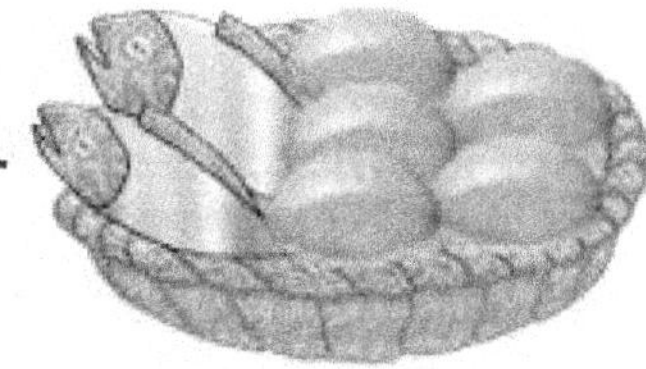

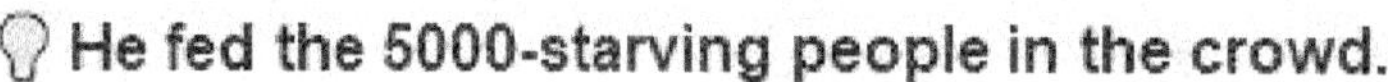

Did you know this?
Jesus shed His Holy
7
Side was pierced after death
Flogged 39-40 times on back
3
Internal Bleeding
6
Crown of Thorns in scalp
2
Nails pounded into ankles
5
JESUS
Sweated Blood while praying
1
Nails pounded into wrists
4
BLOOD for us 7 times

Jesus even went into hell in our place. If I comprehend the Scriptures correctly, He dragged all those sins of ours to hell before Father God resurrected Him on the 3rd day.

If we agree to do the following things, then those sins can be left in hell, with our debt fully paid by Jesus.

🙏 Repent of our sins.

🙏 Ask forgiveness from Jesus or Almighty God for each of our sins. List them out, as many as you can recall.

🙏 Believe that Jesus was our Messiah who died on the Cross in our place, and He rose again on the third day.

🙏 Accept Jesus as our Savior AND our Lord (i.e., our King).

🙏 Do your best not to repeat those same sins. If you do, repent sincerely and ask for the forgiveness of Jesus or Almighty God.

In other words, you need to pray the Sinner's Prayer. Here is one example of the Sinner's Prayer below.

Dear Lord Jesus, I know that I am a sinner, and I ask for Your forgiveness. I believe You died for my sins and rose from the dead. I turn from my sins and invite You to come into my heart and life. I want to trust and follow You as my Lord and Savior. -- GOOGLE QUOTE

Psalm 103:11 For as high as the heavens are above the earth, so great is his love for those who fear him; 12 as far as the east is from the west, so far has he removed our transgressions from us. (NIV)

If we are **SAVED**, our name gets written in the Lamb's Book of Life. That means instead of having to serve an eternal life sentence in hell, we get to reside in Heaven with the Triune God, the Angels, Abraham, King David, the 11 Disciples, Apostle Paul, John the Baptist, Moses, Enoch, other honored elders, and all our other fellow Believers.

If we are SAVED, then we can **PLEAD THE BLOOD**. In other words, when we stand or kneel in front of Almighty God and Jesus for our life review, the Blood of Jesus will cover the book that contains our long list of sins. Since our respective books will be covered with His Holy Blood, we will be ushered into Heaven to live a wonderful eternal life.

🙏 According to people who have experienced NDEs, we will all be around the age of 30 with no infirmities and no need for glasses, hearing aids, pacemakers, seeing-eye dogs, wheelchairs, etc. We will be completely healthy with no reason to sigh, cry, or grieve.

🙏 If we are younger than 30, we can continue to grow.

🙏 Regardless of whether the child died due to miscarriage, at a young age, or aborted, they are in the Third Heaven having a blast playing with the Angels and the tame animals of all types. They are lovingly and eagerly waiting, with forgiving hearts, to reunite with their birth parents.

🙏 We will not be sitting around playing harps and floating on a cloud. There is plenty for us to see, do, and participate in. If we have a talent for music, writing, painting, or other artistic endeavors, we can further foster it. If we love learning, there is a massive library with plenty to discover and explore. If we have an eye for beauty, we will see colors we have never heard of, walk on streets of gold, enjoy living in our mansion, etc.

🙏 We can teleport to whatever part of Heaven we wish to see. Every question we have ever pondered will be instantly answered.

🙏 If we had beloved pets on Earth, we would see them again in Heaven.

🙏 Best of all, we can see and worship the face of Father God. We can hug, talk with, or sit at the feet of Jesus.

🙏 We will also meet our Guardian Angel(s). Be aware that the Angels do not want ever to be worshipped. Their job is always to point us toward worshipping and adoring God.

However ...

Suppose we do not pray that Sinner's Prayer, we will be held accountable for our sins on the day of Judgment. When that time comes, Jesus will read our hearts and judge accordingly. All thoughts can be heard in Heaven as if you yelled them for all to hear. Recording Angels record every thought we have ever thought, every word we have ever said, and every deed we have ever done. Do you really want to take that risk by not accepting His FREE GIFT?

If we are not SAVED and Jesus reads and finds your heart full of arrogance, unrepentance, pride, unforgiveness, etc., then we will not be allowed through Heaven's gates.

1. What are all the reasons why Jesus kept dropping the cross?

2. What did Jesus tell the women who were crying about his situation? What message was He trying to get across to them?

3. Who was the one who helped Jesus carry the cross? List all the reasons why you think he agreed to do this.

4. Why do you think Jesus refused to drink the numbing liquid offered to him by the Roman soldiers?

5. Describe the place where the crucifixion of Jesus took place.

6. Describe in what way this prophecy or foreshadowing about Jesus explains that he will be hung high on a cross.

> **Isaiah 52:13 Behold, my servant shall deal prudently, he shall be exalted and extolled, and be very high. (KJV)**

7. In Isaiah 50:6, Isaiah prophesied some of the tortures the Messiah would have to endure. What were they?

> **Isaiah 50:6 I gave my back to the smiters, and my cheeks to them that plucked off the hair: I hid not my face from shame and spitting. (KJV)**

8. Look through Chapter 2's list of 20 physical traumas Jesus had to endure. Describe five of them that disturb you the most. Please explain.

9. Can you think of any other physical traumas Jesus had to endure that were not listed? What would those have been?

10. Look through Chapter 2's list of emotional traumas Jesus had to endure. Describe five of them that disturb you the most. Please explain.

11. Can you think of any other emotional traumas Jesus had to endure that were not listed? What would those have been?

12. How do you think Jesus managed to be strong and loving enough to endure what He did for our sakes? In other words, how did He manage to allow His Love for us override His fear?

13. In what ways did Jesus humble Himself as a servant? See the latter part of Chapter 2 to reference the four examples listed by the author.

14. What is your theory of how Jesus managed to absorb all of our sins within His body as He hung on the cross? What do you think happened to those sins afterward?

15. How do we get our names listed in the Lamb's Book of Life? Do you feel confident that your name is part of that list? Why or why not? If not, what can you do to change that?

16. Knowing that the Recording Angels document all our thoughts, words, and deeds (good and bad), does it motivate you to try to make sure your thoughts, words, and deeds are more positive than negative? If not, why not? If so, in what ways are you vigilant or not vigilant about your own behavior?

ROMAN SOLDIERS CAST LOTS FOR JESUS' CLOTHES.

Crucifixion of Jesus Christ – our Savior & Lord

Examine 4 Gospels for Clues (KJV)

Matthew 27:35	Mark 15:24-25	Luke 23:34	John 19:23-24
35 And they crucified him, and parted his garments, casting lots: that it might be fulfilled which was spoken by the prophet, **They parted my garments among them, and upon my vesture did they cast lots.**	24 And when they had crucified him, they parted his garments, casting lots upon them, what every man should take. 25 And it was the third hour (i.e, 9 AM), and they crucified him.	34 ... And they parted his raiment, and cast lots. 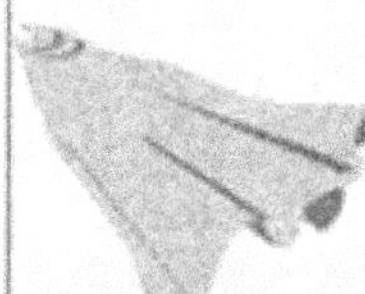 	23 Then the soldiers, when they had crucified Jesus, took his garments, and made four parts, to every soldier a part; and also his coat: now the coat was without seam, woven from the top throughout. 24 They said therefore among themselves, **Let us not rend it, but cast lots for it, whose it shall be:** that the scripture might be fulfilled, which saith, **They parted my raiment among them, and for my vesture they did cast lots.** These things therefore the soldiers did.

King David

REMEZ – Hidden Message
Psalm 22:18 They part my garments among them, and cast lots upon my vesture. (KJV)

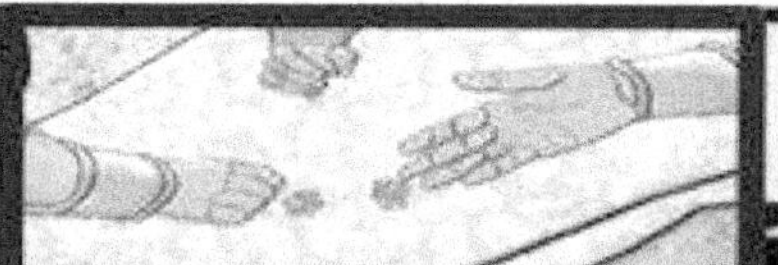

How did the Romans cast lots for the clothes of Jesus?

"The practice of casting lots usually involved sticks or stones with markings or dice. The sticks or stones or dice were thrown into an area and read to determine the winner. The practice of rolling dice or flipping a coin is similar to the casting of lots in Bible times. When the soldiers cast lots for Jesus' garments, they left Him, quite literally, with no possessions. Truly, Jesus became poor so that we might become rich (Luke 9:58; 2 Corinthians 8:9)."

Luke 9:58 And Jesus said unto him, Foxes have holes, and birds of the air have nests; but the Son of man hath not where to lay his head. (KJV)

2 Corinthians 8:9 For ye know the grace of our Lord Jesus Christ, that, though he was rich, yet for your sakes he became poor, that ye through his poverty might be rich.

Be aware that Jesus was probably wholly naked. The Roman soldiers exposed Him for all to see and humiliate. For our sake, He endured this and more.

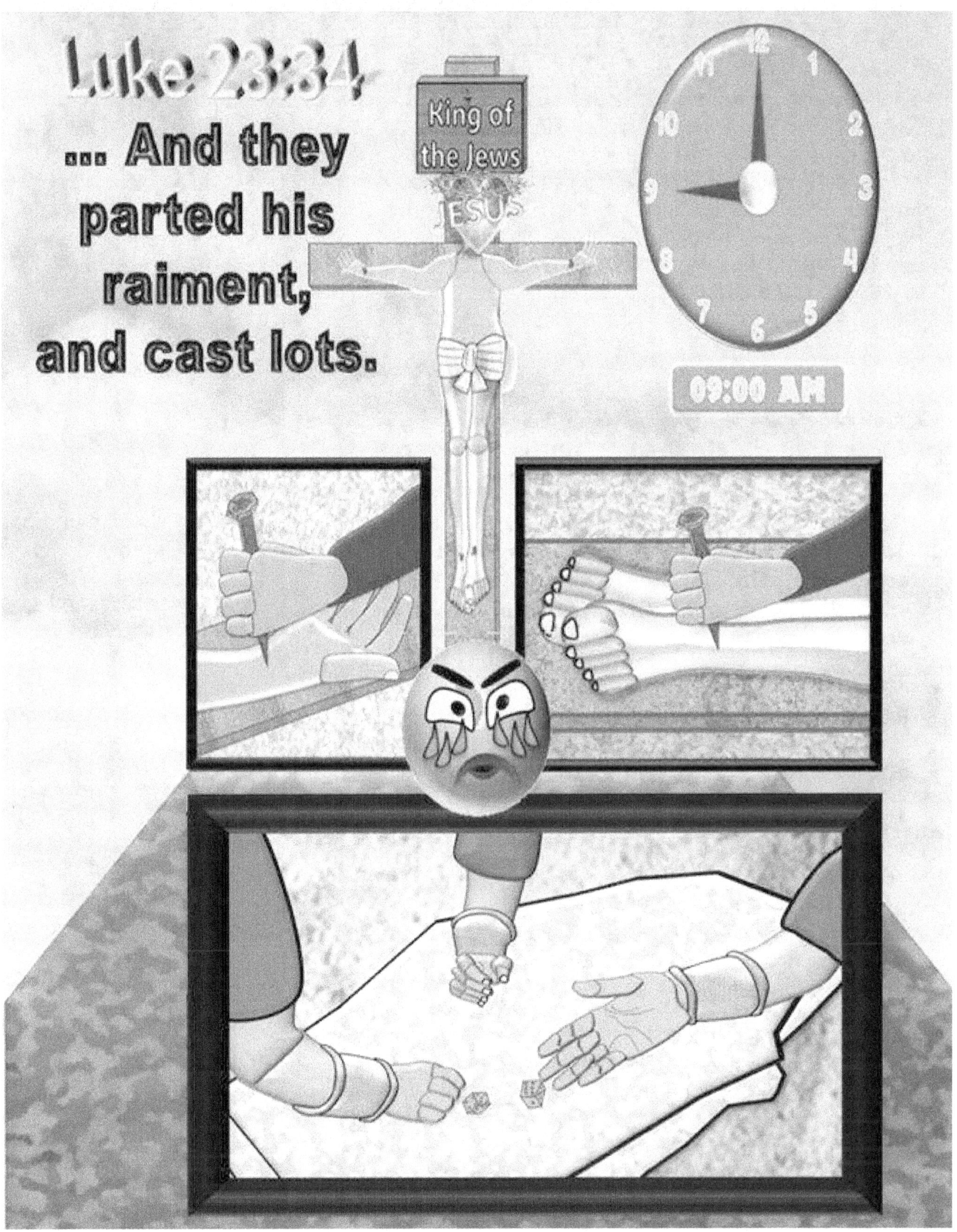

A 'KING OF THE JEWS' SIGN WAS POSTED ABOVE JESUS' HEAD.

Governor Pontius Pilate had the Roman Soldiers post a sign near the top of the cross that indicated that Jesus was the **KING OF THE JEWS**. The most detailed account was listed in the Book of **John 19:19-22** as seen below. The other three Gospels also referenced this sign in **Matthew 27:37**, **Mark 15:26**, and **Luke 23:38**.

John 19:9 Pilate had a notice prepared and fastened to the cross. It read: Jesus of Nazareth, the king of the jews.

John 19:20 Many of the Jews read this sign, for the place where Jesus was crucified was near the city, and the sign was written in Aramaic, Latin and Greek.

John 19:21 The chief priests of the Jews protested to Pilate, "Do not write 'The King of the Jews,' but that this man claimed to be king of the Jews."

John 19:22 Pilate answered, "What I have written, I have written."

GOOGLE QUOTE: "The official language of the Roman empire was **Latin**, which was used for official documents and communication."

NEXT GOOGLE QUOTE: 'What language did they speak in Jesus' time? **Aramaic** was the everyday language of Jesus and his people. **Greek** was the common language of business and the Gentiles. **Hebrew** was the language of educated Jews in Jesus' time. The books of the Old Testament were written in **Hebrew**.

FYI – "The proper Hebrew name for Jesus is **Yeshua**, which means SALVATION."
- From Free Messianic Bible.com *(See Bibliography for the link.)*

On YouTube, you see this name pronounced as: **Yeh-shoo-uh**) *with the stress on the middle syllable.*

From One For Israel.org,
"**JESUS**
= **YESHUA**
= **CHRIST**
(Greek word for Messiah)
= **MESSIAH**."
(See Bibliography for the link.)

It was common for the Romans to place a sign near the top of the cross that listed the charges of each crucified person. The Romans called this sign a TITLON. Here is its definition.

Several sources listed in the Bibliography proclaimed that Pontius Pilate, either intentionally or accidentally, proclaimed **Jesus as God** in the Hebrew translation of the Titlon sign posted on the cross. There are also a few sources that disagree with this idea. On the chance that it was true, here is a potential **Remez or hidden message** that would explain why the Jewish elders were overly upset by the wording of the accusation on the sign.

As stated in the sources, do be aware that "Hebrew is read from right to left."

English Translation: Yeshua aka Jesus the Nazarite *and* the King of the Jews

4 3 2 1
ישוע הנצרי ומלך היהודים
ל ה ר ה
1 ל
2 ה
3 ר
4 ה
Y
H
W
H
YHWH
Old Testament name for God

3 Google quotes
What is an acrostic in the Bible?

"Some biblical poetry is written using acrostics, meaning that each stanza or verse (or sometimes each half verse) begins with a different letter of the alphabet in a specific sequence, usually alphabetic. Acrostics are found in the books of Psalms, Proverbs, and Lamentations."

"There are 24 verses in the Hebrew Old Testament which contain the acrostic spelled forwards (i.e. spelled YHWH)."

"There are also 34 verses in the Hebrew Old Testament which contain the acrostic spelled backwards (i.e. spelled HWHY)."

What is the acronym YHWH?
"Yahweh, name for the God of the Israelites, representing the biblical pronunciation of "YHWH," the Hebrew name revealed to Moses in the book of Exodus. The name YHWH, consisting of the sequence of consonants Yod, Heh, Waw, and Heh, is known as the tetragrammaton."

MOSES

TWO THIEVES NAILED TO CROSSES ON EITHER SIDE OF JESUS.

Crucifixion of Jesus Christ – our Savior & Lord

BIBLE CLUES (KJV) ??? Examine 4 Gospels for Clues (KJV) ??? BIBLE CLUES (KJV)

Matthew 27:38	Mark 15:27-28	Luke 23:32-33	John 19:18
38 Then were there two thieves crucified with him, one on the right hand, and another on the left.	**27** And with him they crucify two thieves; the one on his right hand, and the other on his left. **28** And the scripture was fulfilled, which saith, And he was numbered with the transgressors.	**32** And there were also two other, malefactors, led with him to be put to death. **33** And when they were come to the place, which is called Calvary, there they crucified him, and the malefactors, one on the right hand, and the other on the left.	**18** Where they crucified him, and two other with him, on either side one, and Jesus in the midst.

Isaiah 53:12 Therefore will I divide him a portion with the great, and he shall divide the spoil with the strong; because he hath poured out his soul unto death: and he was numbered with the transgressors; and he bare the sin of many, and made intercession for the transgressors. (KJV)

Psalm 22:11 Be not far from me; for trouble is near; for there is none to help. 12 Many bulls have compassed me: strong bulls of Bashan have beset me round. 13 They gaped upon me with their mouths, as a ravening and a roaring lion. ... 16 For dogs have compassed me: the assembly of the wicked have inclosed me: ... (KJV)

Isaiah 53:3 He is despised and rejected of men; a man of sorrows, and acquainted with grief: and we hid as it were our faces from him; he was despised, and we esteemed him not. (KJV)

Isaiah 53:7 He was oppressed, and he was afflicted, yet he opened not his mouth: he is brought as a lamb to the slaughter, and as a sheep before her shearers is dumb, so he openeth not his mouth. (KJV)

JESUS MOCKED BY CROWD

Crucifixion of Jesus Christ – our Savior & Lord

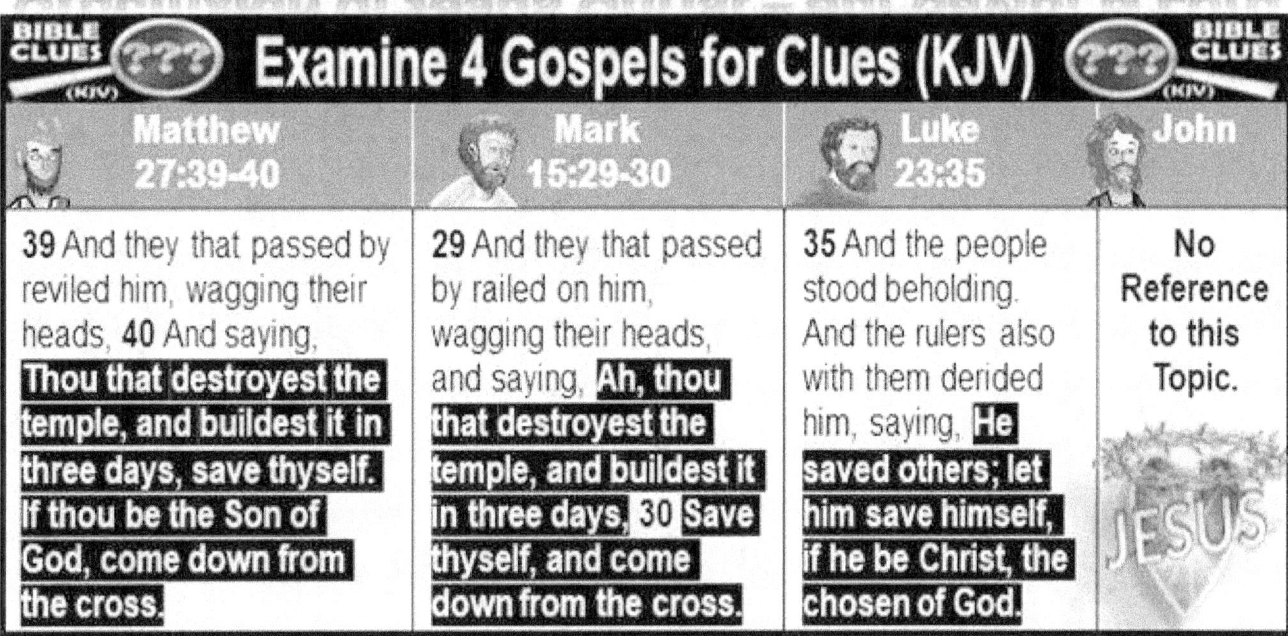

Examine 4 Gospels for Clues (KJV)

Matthew 27:39-40	Mark 15:29-30	Luke 23:35	John
39 And they that passed by reviled him, wagging their heads, 40 And saying, **Thou that destroyest the temple, and buildest it in three days, save thyself. If thou be the Son of God, come down from the cross.**	29 And they that passed by railed on him, wagging their heads, and saying, **Ah, thou that destroyest the temple, and buildest it in three days, 30 Save thyself, and come down from the cross.**	35 And the people stood beholding. And the rulers also with them derided him, saying, **He saved others; let him save himself, if he be Christ, the chosen of God.**	No Reference to this Topic.

In addition to all the other stressors, Jesus had the humiliation of crowds of people seeing His privates (most likely) and his shredded, bleeding skin. He also had to see the unsympathetic, mocking faces of people and hear how they made fun of Him with loud, jeering voices.

JESUS MOCKED BY PHARISEES

Crucifixion of Jesus Christ – our Savior & Lord

BIBLE CLUES (KJV) ??? Examine 4 Gospels for Clues (KJV) ??? BIBLE CLUES (KJV)

Matthew 27:41-43	Mark 15:31-32	Luke 23:35	John
41 Likewise also the chief priests mocking him, with the scribes and elders, said, 42 He saved others; himself he cannot save. If he be the King of Israel, let him now come down from the cross, and we will believe him. 43 He trusted in God; let him deliver him now, if he will have him: for he said, I am the Son of God.	31 Likewise also the chief priests mocking said among themselves with the scribes, He saved others; himself he cannot save. 32 Let Christ the King of Israel descend now from the cross, that we may see and believe. …	35 … And the rulers also with them derided him, saying, He saved others; let him save himself, if he be Christ, the chosen of God.	No Reference to this Topic. King of the Jews JESUS

REMEZ – Hidden Message

Psalm 22:7 All they that see me laugh me to scorn: they shoot out the lip, they shake the head, saying, 8 He trusted on the Lord that he would deliver him: let him deliver him, seeing he delighted in him. (KJV)

It certainly appeared that the Pharisees had a prescribed view of what a true Messiah would and would not do.

You can't be the Messiah as you don't fit my boxed-in view of the interaction between God and this man who claims to be His Son. How can that be true since God did not deliver you from the cross but allowed you to die?

Crucifixion of Jesus Christ – our Savior & Lord

BIBLE CLUES (KJV) ??? Examine 4 Gospels for Clues (KJV) ??? BIBLE CLUES (KJV)	
Matthew, Mark, & John	Luke 23:36-37
No Reference to this Topic.	36 And the soldiers also mocked him, coming to him, and offering him vinegar, 37 And saying, **If thou be the king of the Jews, save thyself.**

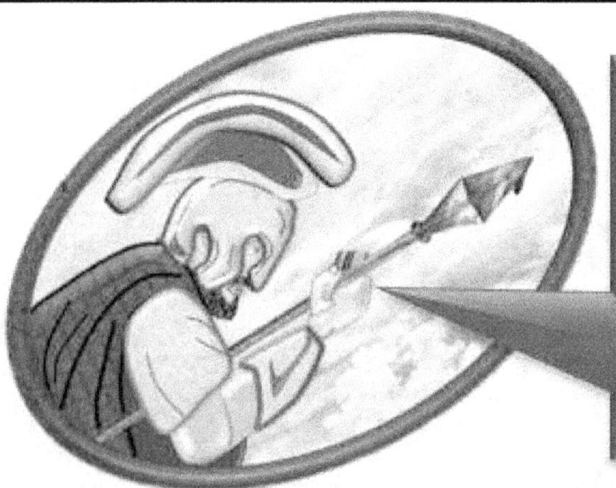

If thou be
the king of
the Jews,
save thyself.

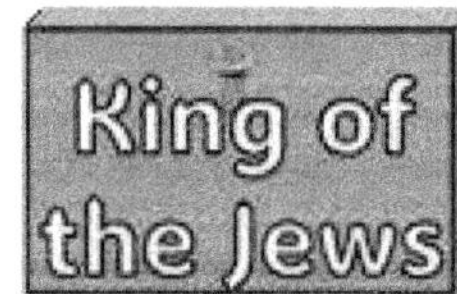

JESUS MOCKED BY 2 THIEVES

Crucifixion of Jesus Christ – our Savior & Lord

Examine 4 Gospels for Clues (KJV)

Matthew 27:44	Mark 15:32	Luke 23:39-40	John
44 The thieves also, which were crucified with him, cast the same in his teeth.	**32** ... And they that were crucified with him reviled him.	**39** And one of the malefactors which were hanged railed on him, saying, **If thou be Christ, save thyself and us.** **40** But the other answering rebuked him, saying, **Dost not thou fear God, seeing thou art in the same condemnation?**	No Reference to this Topic.

aka MOB MENTALITY

In two distinct instances, Jesus had to face the act of Psychological Warfare, also known as Mob Mentality. The Sanhedrin bribed or convinced the Jews to vote to free Barabbas and crucify Jesus. They also encouraged others to mock Jesus' suffering and predicament at the Cross.

SEPARATION FROM THE HERD

At the Garden of Gethsemane, the Sanhedrin managed to separate Jesus from the Disciples and His adoring Followers to arrest Him with the help of Judas. In other words, they were able to separate Him from the Herd so that they could manage to try Him, get a GUILTY verdict, and then witness Jesus getting crucified.

1. Why do you think the Roman soldiers cast lots for the clothes of Jesus?

2. What do you think the Roman soldiers did with those clothes if they happened to win them? Do you think it would have made the Roman soldiers modify their future behavior (either good or bad)?

3. Describe what was listed on the sign hanging above Jesus' head. What languages were utilized for the wording of that sign?

4. Why did the Pharisees want the wording of that sign changed?

5. Why do you think Pilate refused to change the wording on the sign?

6. What name do the Jewish people use for Christ instead of Jesus? What is their translation for the name they have chosen to call Him by? (See Chapter 5)

7. Study the page in Chapter 5 describing YHWH and acrostics from the Bible. What did you learn from that page?

8. What do you know about the men hanging on crosses on either side of Jesus?

9. What did the crowds say who mocked Jesus?

10. What did the Pharisees say who mocked Jesus?

11. What did the Roman soldiers say who mocked Jesus?

12. What did the thieves say who mocked Jesus?

13. Do you agree that much of that mocking took place due to the Psychological Warfare technique known as mob mentality? If so, when else have you witnessed that technique being used either in your life, school, place of employment, in movies or television shows, or on the News?

14. Why do you think one thief defended Jesus and the other one continued to mock Jesus?

15. See the Remez statements listed on the last page of Chapter 6. Which Bible verse or verses did you find to be the most significant? Why is that?

SUNLIGHT FOR CRUCIFIXION MORNING & DARK AS NIGHT FROM 12 PM TO 3 PM

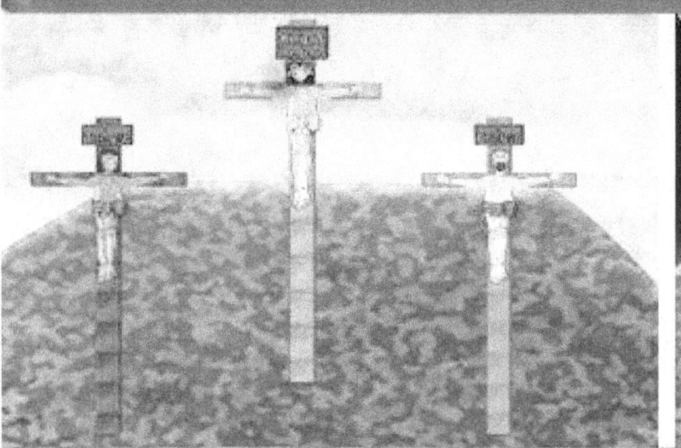

Jesus did not speak all morning.

10:00 AM

End of 1st Hour on Cross

About 10 AM on Friday, Bright as day

Cavalry: Golgotha – The Place of a Skull

11:00 AM

End of 2nd Hour on Cross

About 11 AM on Friday, Bright as day

Cavalry: Golgotha – The Place of a Skull

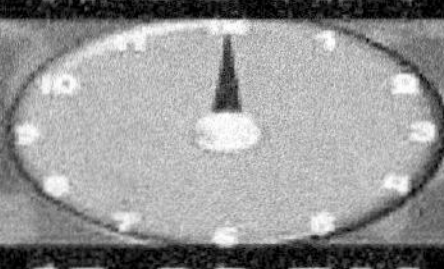

12:00 PM

End of 3rd Hour on Cross

About 12 PM Friday, Bright as day

Cavalry: Golgotha – The Place of a Skull

Jesus did not speak until 3 PM.

1:00 PM

End of 4th Hour on Cross

About 1 PM on Friday, Dark as night

Cavalry: Golgotha – The Place of a Skull

2:00 PM

End of 5th Hour on Cross

About 2 PM on Friday, Dark as night

Cavalry: Golgotha – The Place of a Skull

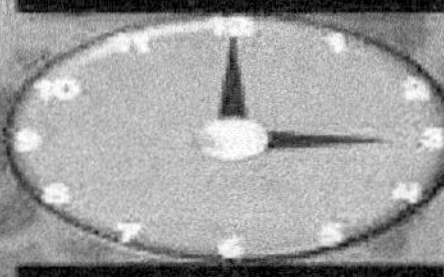

3:00 PM

End of 6th Hour on Cross

About 3 PM on Friday, Dark as night

Cavalry: Golgotha – The Place of a Skull

REMEZ – Hidden Message

Amos 8:9 And it shall come to pass in that day, saith the Lord God, that I will cause the sun to go down at noon, and I will darken the earth in the clear day. (KJV)

Fact about Inventors of Crucifixion?

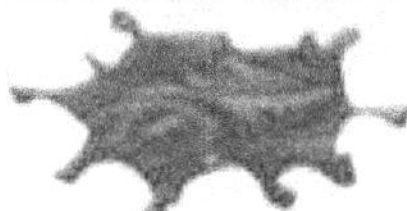
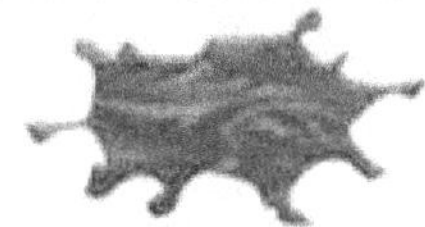

Cahleen Shrier, Ph.D. quote

Who invented Crucifixion and when?

"Crucifixion was invented by the Persians between 300-400 B.C. It is quite possibly the most painful death ever invented by humankind. The English language derives the word 'excruciating' from crucifixion, acknowledging it as a form of slow, painful suffering."

excruciating

Crucifixion of Jesus Christ – our Savior & Lord

Examine 4 Gospels for Clues (KJV)

Matthew 27:45	Mark 15:33	Luke 23:44-45	John
45 Now from the sixth hour there was darkness over all the land unto the ninth hour.	33 And when the sixth hour was come, there was darkness over the whole land until the ninth hour.	44 And it was about the sixth hour, and there was a darkness over all the earth until the ninth hour. 45 And the sun was darkened, and the veil of the temple was rent in the midst.	No Reference to this Topic.

The whole world went dark. Jesus did not speak from 12-3 PM

End of 4th Hour on Cross — **1:00 PM**	About 1 PM on Friday, Dark as night	Cavalry: Golgotha – The Place of a Skull
End of 5th Hour on Cross — **2:00 PM**	About 2 PM on Friday, Dark as night	Cavalry: Golgotha – The Place of a Skull
End of 6th Hour on Cross — **3:00 PM**	About 3 PM on Friday, Dark as night	Cavalry: Golgotha – The Place of a Skull

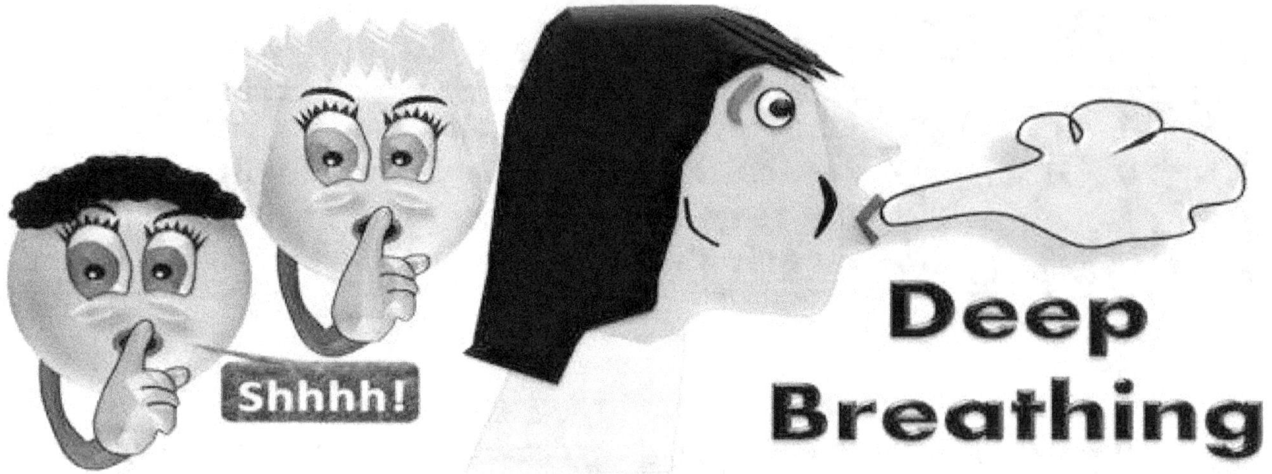

Jesus did not talk during the first six hours hanging on the Cross because He fulfilled Scripture and followed His Father's will. He also had to focus on absorbing and assimilating all of our Sins. Finally, it would have been excruciating to inhale, exhale, talk, and breathe simultaneously. See the description below.

"Normally, to breathe in, the diaphragm (the large muscle that separates the chest cavity from the abdominal cavity) must move down. This enlarges the chest cavity and air automatically moves into the lungs (inhalation). To exhale, the diaphragm rises up, which compresses the air in the lungs and forces the air out (exhalation).

As Jesus hangs on the cross, the weight of His body pulls down on the diaphragm and the air moves into His lungs and remains there. Jesus must push up on His nailed feet (causing more pain) to exhale."

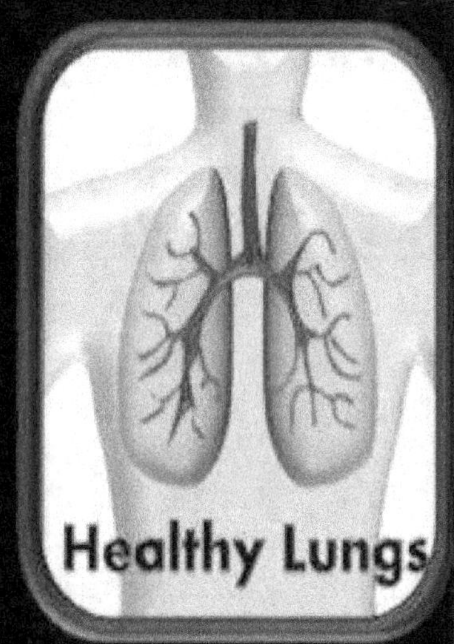

1. To repeat this particular Remez quote from the book of Isaiah, what are all the reasons you can think of why Jesus did not talk during most of the trials and the Crucifixion?

2. Check out the timeline below. The Prophet Isaiah, who lived about 700 hundred years before Christ, provided a lot of foreshadowing statements and prophecies about the Crucifixion. Take note of when the torture method of Crucifixion was invented. How could Isaiah and the other Prophets have known?

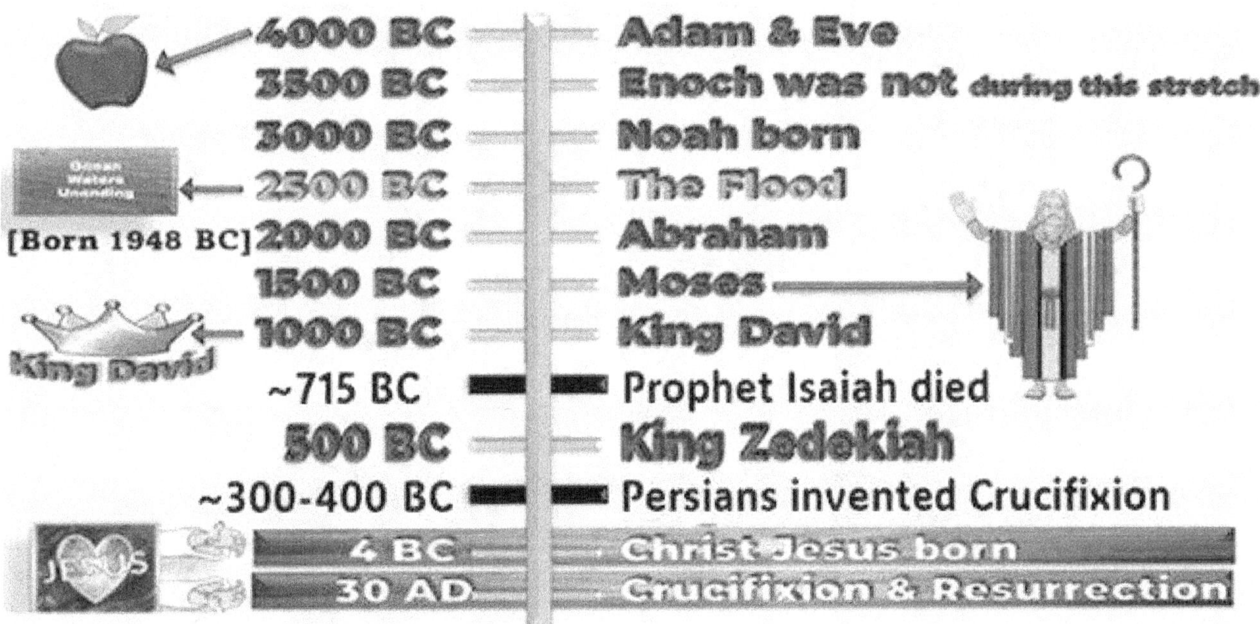

3. What did you discover about the origin of the word EXCRUTIATING? Describe various ways that demonstrated the truth of that for Jesus.

4. When the world went dark from 12 noon to 3 PM, do you think the Pharisees or the Roman soldiers speculated that perhaps their role in killing Jesus had any connection to this strange phenomenon?

5. Why was it such a hardship to breathe and talk at the same time for Jesus?

Jesus only made seven statements from the Cross.

Chapter 13: “Father, Forgive them for they know not what they do.”

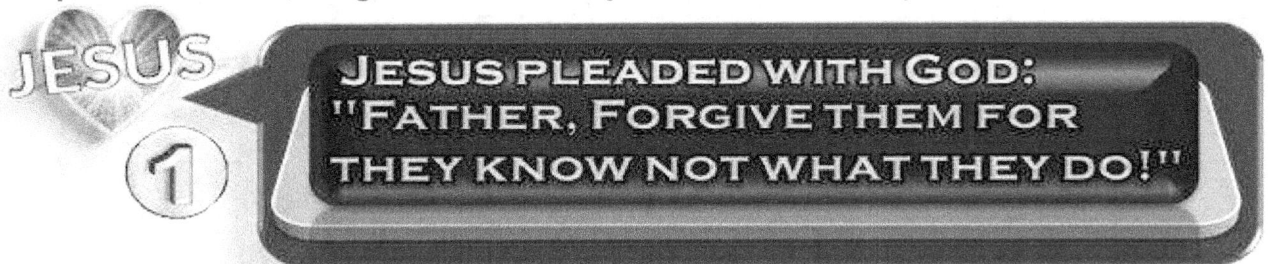

The Book of Luke was the only Gospel that references this speech by Jesus.

Crucifixion of Jesus Christ – our Savior & Lord

Examine 4 Gospels for Clues (KJV)

Matthew, Mark, & John	Luke 23:34
No Reference to this Topic.	34 Then said Jesus, **Father, forgive them; for they know not what they do.** And they parted his raiment, and cast lots.

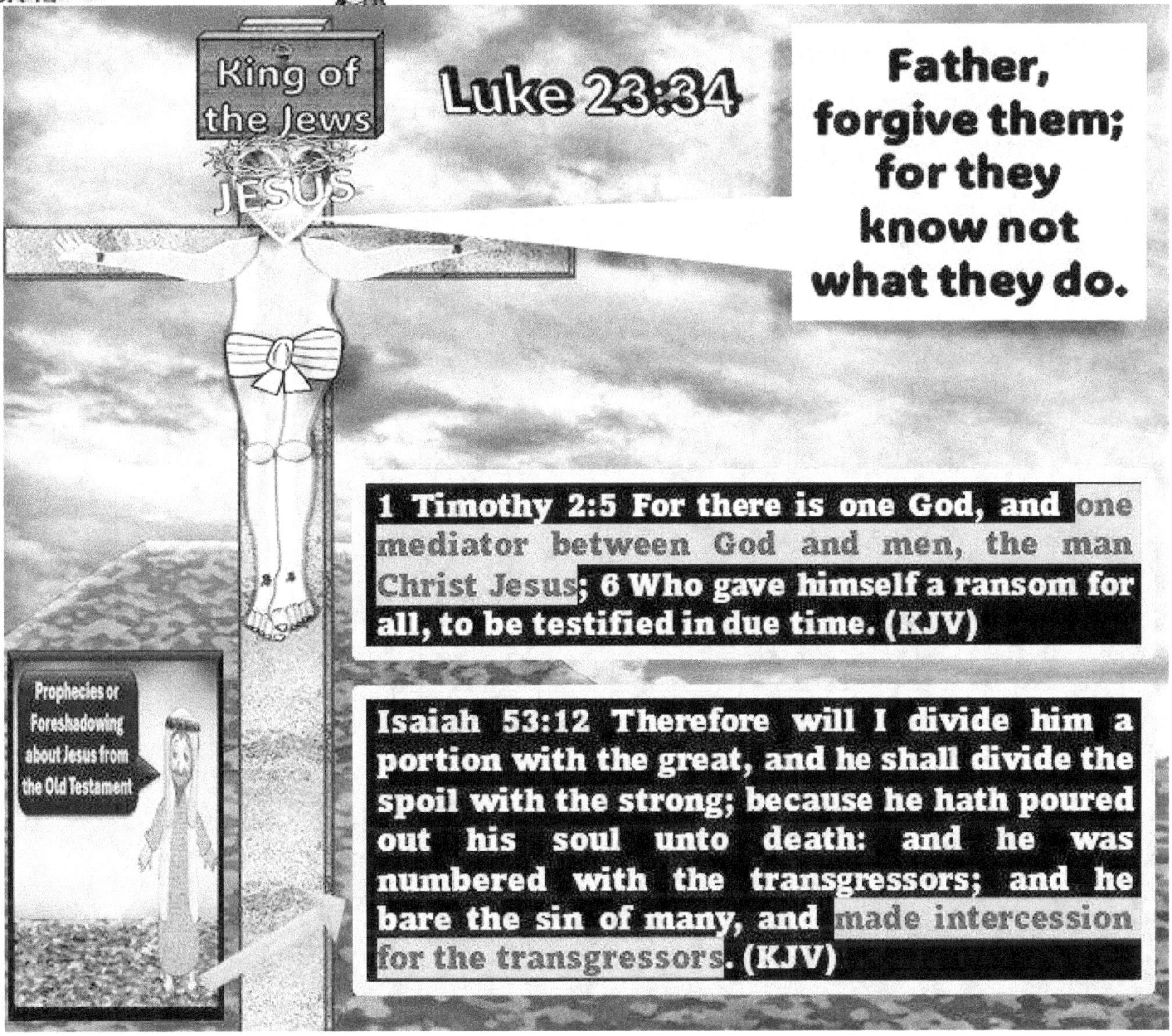

King of the Jews

JESUS

Matthew 18:11 For the Son of man is come to save that which was lost.

12 How think ye? if a man have an hundred sheep, and one of them be gone astray, doth he not leave the ninety and nine, and goeth into the mountains, and seeketh that which is gone astray?

13 And if so be that he find it, verily I say unto you, he rejoiceth more of that sheep, than of the ninety and nine which went not astray.

14 Even so it is not the will of your Father which is in heaven, that one of these little ones should perish. (KJV)

FORGIVE THEM

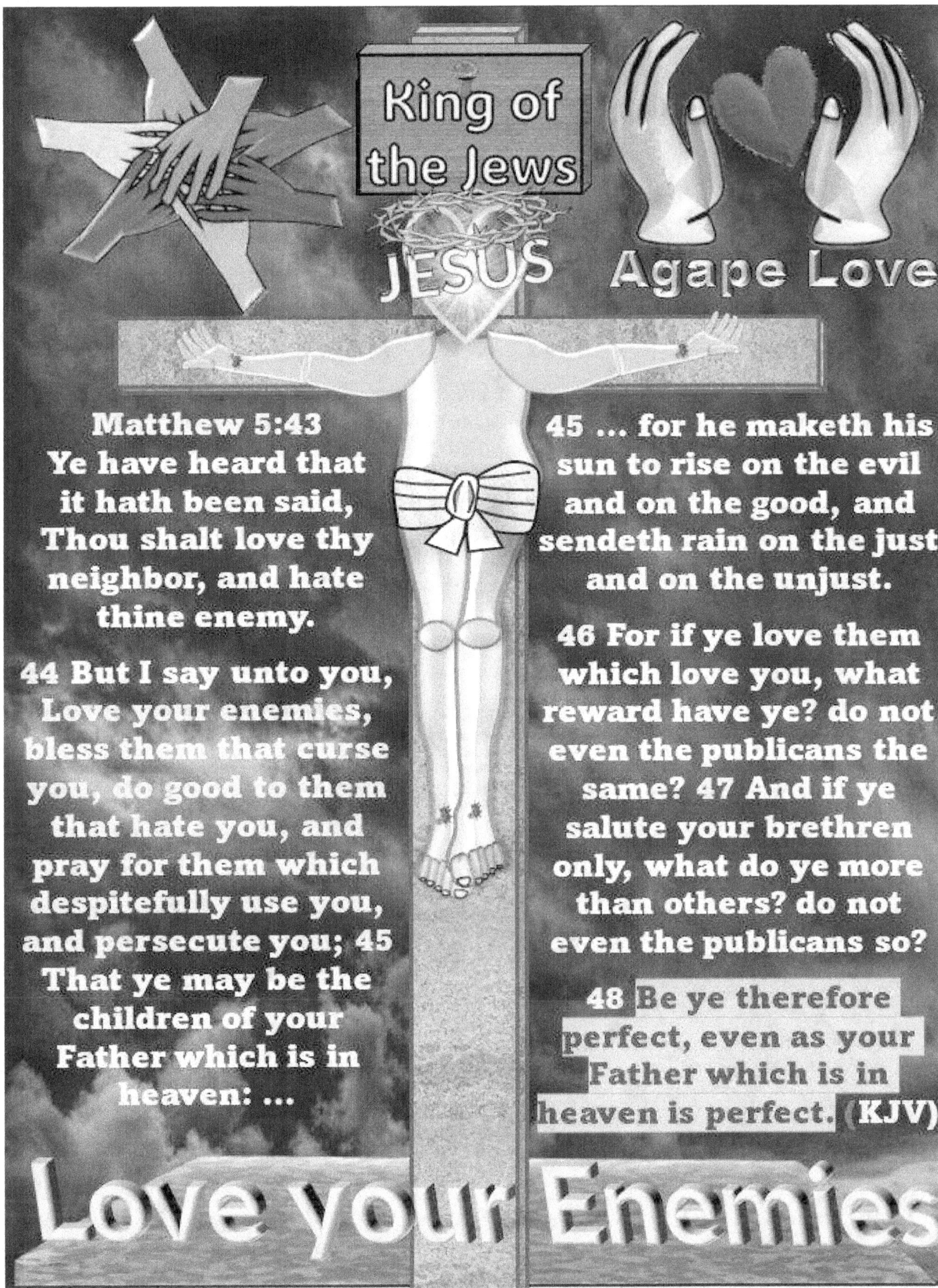
King of
the Jews
JESUS
Agape Love
Matthew 5:43 Ye have heard that it hath been said, Thou shalt love thy neighbor, and hate thine enemy.
44 But I say unto you, Love your enemies, bless them that curse you, do good to them that hate you, and pray for them which despitefully use you, and persecute you; 45 That ye may be the children of your Father which is in heaven: ...
45 ... for he maketh his sun to rise on the evil and on the good, and sendeth rain on the just and on the unjust.
46 For if ye love them which love you, what reward have ye? do not even the publicans the same? 47 And if ye salute your brethren only, what do ye more than others? do not even the publicans so?
48 Be ye therefore perfect, even as your Father which is in heaven is perfect. (KJV)
Love your Enemies

Crucifixion of Jesus Christ – our Savior & Lord

Examine 4 Gospels for Clues (KJV)

Matthew, Mark, & John	Luke 23:39-43

No Reference to this Topic.

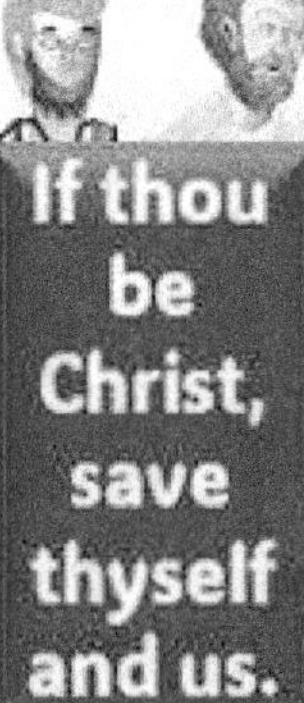

39 And one of the malefactors which were hanged railed on him, saying, **If thou be Christ, save thyself and us.**

40 But the other answering rebuked him, saying, **Dost not thou fear God, seeing thou art in the same condemnation? 41 And we indeed justly; for we receive the due reward of our deeds: but this man hath done nothing amiss.**

42 And he said unto Jesus, **Lord, remember me when thou comest into thy kingdom.**

43 And Jesus said unto him, **Verily I say unto thee, Today shalt thou be with me in paradise.**

As you know, two thieves were hung on a cross - one on either side of our Lord Jesus. The Bible does not designate the positions. I am placing the unrepentant thief on Jesus' left and the repentant thief on Jesus' right.

On this Friday morning, when the Roman soldiers crucified these three men, many people began to mock and revile Jesus. People passing by mocked Jesus. The Pharisees mocked Jesus. The Roman soldiers mocked Jesus. Even the two thieves mocked Jesus.

So, when did the thief on the right have a change of heart? The Bible does not say. Of course, as John stated in **John 21:25**, if the Bible included every detail about Jesus's lifetime on the earth, the Bible would have ended up being hundreds and hundreds of pages long. That leaves us to read between the lines and guess what it did not document.

John 21:25 And there are also many other things which Jesus did, the which, if they should be written every one, I suppose that even the world itself could not contain the books that should be written. Amen. (KJV)

In picturing the thief on the right, when he was not focused on his physical pain and trying to inhale and exhale the best he could, he would be trying to distract his brain with his immediate surroundings.

First, he might have noticed that Jesus handled all the mockery with grace and a sad smile. Jesus did not appear angry, disgusted, or even disquieted by the cruel things that everyone was saying. Maybe even at one point, Jesus turned His head to His right and lovingly looked into the thief's eyes. Jesus might have tried to do the same with the thief hanging to His left. Even if He did, it appears the other thief was not receptive to Jesus' overtures.

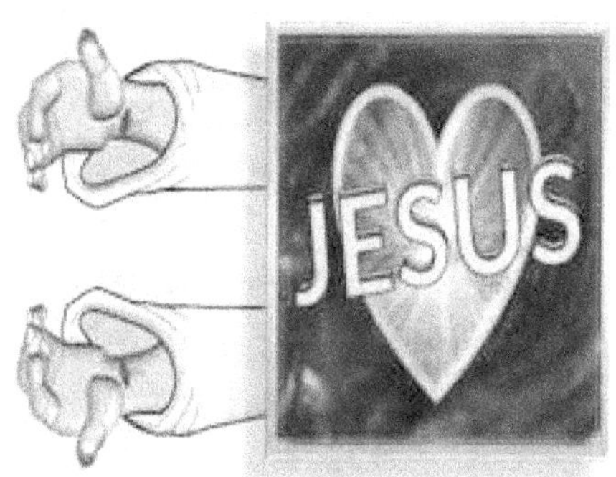

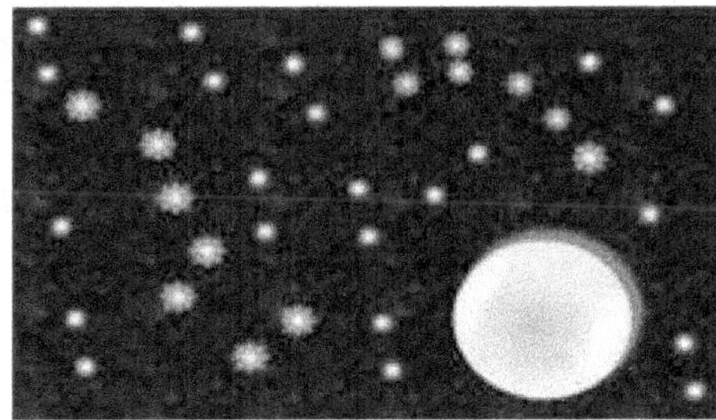

Secondly, the thief on the right would have been frightened, along with the crowd below him, when the sky went dark at high noon. The fact that it was dark as night for those three hours must have caused many superstitious people to wonder if this might be the way that God Almighty was expressing His displeasure that the Roman soldiers crucified His only Son as if He was only a common criminal.

Thirdly, if the thief on the right could read, he would have been able to take note of the sign above Jesus' head indicating that He was the King of the Jews. Even if he couldn't read, he would have heard the people gossiping about what they read on that sign.

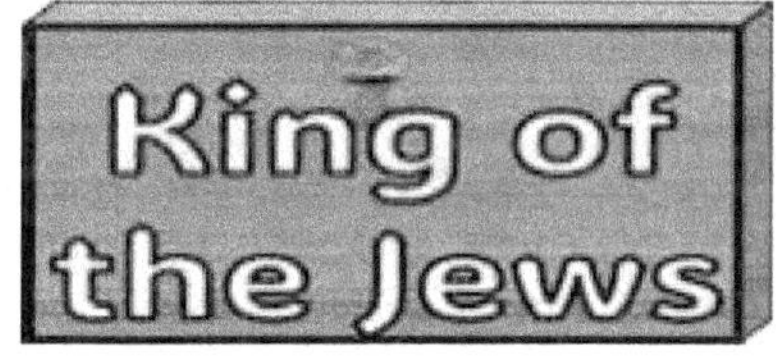

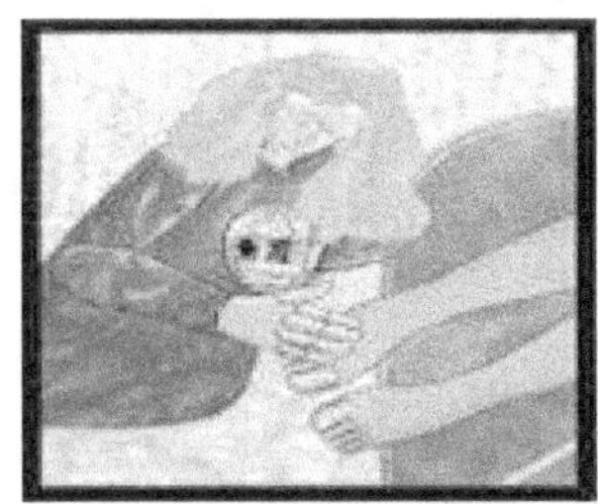

Fourthly, probably everyone had heard that Jesus healed lepers, the blind, the dead, the sick, and paralytics. He had even brought a man back to life. The thief on the right might have concluded that Jesus might indeed be the Son of God Almighty. This thief may have even attended one or more of Jesus' preaching to the multitude out of curiosity and to pick a pocket or two along with his fellow thieves.

So, when the thief on the right heard his long-time thieving buddy make such a cruel remark, he not only wanted to defend Jesus but also hint at or clarify that he deeply regretted he had lived weeks, months, or years of his life as a thief. His thieving buddy had said, in a cruel, sarcastic tone, "**If thou be Christ, save thyself and us.**" It was obvious by his word choice of saying '**IF**' that he didn't believe Jesus was the Son of God.

The thief on the right was so convicted by what he had heard, seen, and processed that he gasped, "**Dost not thou fear God, seeing thou art in the same condemnation? And we indeed justly; for we receive the due reward of our deeds: but this man hath done nothing amiss.**"

The now fully repentant thief began to sincerely regret all the bad things he had done. One or more people he had robbed might have been in the crowd below. Perhaps he mouthed the words to them, "**I am sorry for what I did to you.**" Even if none of them were present, he might have wished that he could apologize to each one and perhaps even offer to work for them in some manner, without pay, to make up for the way he had defrauded them.

For those reading this who have ever prayed the Sinner's Prayer, you likely recognize that this repentant thief was already fulfilling its first half. He publicly recognized and acknowledged that he was a sinner. Internally, he was repenting of those sins and mentally telling them how sorry he was.

It was clear that if the Roman soldiers set the two thieves free from the cross, the thief on Jesus' left likely would have resumed his robbing ways. As for the thief on the right, he might genuinely have been on his way to being a changed man. The Holy Spirit would have been hovering nearby and read this man's contrite heart. He began pouring some of His Spirit into this repentant man.

The clincher was when the contrite thief heard Jesus call out the words, "Father, forgive them; for they know not what they do."

Suddenly, the repentant thief knew what he must do.

The Holy Spirit managed to alert him that Jesus was God's Son. The now repentant thief also would comprehend that this Godly man was allowing Himself to be sacrificed for the sake of all humankind.

So, with heart beating extra fast, he nervously but sincerely called out, "Lord, remember me when thou comest into thy kingdom."

Dear Lord Jesus, I know that I am a sinner, and I ask for Your forgiveness. I believe You died for my sins and rose from the dead. I turn from my sins and invite You to come into my heart and life. I want to trust and follow You as my Lord and Savior. -- GOOGLE QUOTE

Jesus' Loving heart probably swelled with joy. He recognized that this man was ripe to be reborn. He had already stated he was a sinner. Jesus had already scanned through his life and saw the tough breaks he endured and the wrong companion choices he had made that led him into a life of sin. His word choices made it clear that this contrite man accepted Jesus as his Lord and Savior.

So, Jesus, with loving eyes, gasped out His reply, "Verily I say unto thee, Today shalt thou be with me in paradise."

The repentant thief likely felt his eyes tear up with relief and a feeling of joy that he had never experienced in his entire life. Even though his life was soon to end, he felt like a new man. Nobody else would know or be able to recognize that he had been reborn, but Jesus knew. The Holy Spirit also knew, even if this man did not know about the Triune God: God the Father, Son, and Holy Spirit.

Jesus only had five more things He intended to say before dying. After Jesus died, perhaps people continued to criticize and mock the two thieves. The thief on Jesus' left might have said some nasty things back to them. But the thief on the right was too full of this strange feeling of joy and renewal to pay them any mind. He was a changed man.

We have a conundrum or head-scratcher to consider.

From 2nd Timothy, we learn that all Scripture is 'God-breathed.'

> **2 Timothy 3:16** All scripture is given by inspiration of God, and is profitable for doctrine, for reproof, for correction, for instruction in righteousness: **17** That the man of God may be perfect, thoroughly furnished unto all good works. (KJV)

What about the punctuation?

"Is the Comma Inspired? Is the punctuation in the Bible inspired? In the original Greek text of the New Testament there was no punctuation, in fact, there was no spacing between words. Here is a quote from the Greek language expert Michael W. Palmer. "The ancient Greeks did not have any equivalent to our modern device of punctuation. Sentence punctuation was invented several centuries after the time of Christ. The oldest copies of both the Greek New Testament and the Hebrew Old Testament are written with no punctuation."

When the translators of the English Bible translated this verse and others they had to decide where the punctuation should be. The translators themselves were not inspired. God definitely helped them translate the Bible, but the punctuation is not inspired since there was no punctuation in the original manuscripts. Translators made the simple mistake of placing the comma in the wrong position, perhaps because of their traditional beliefs about what happens when you die."

Given that situation, the translators would have seen this:

They would have had to make a punctuation choice about when the thief would have entered Paradise. If they decided that Jesus might have made a quick stop in Paradise to drop the thief off before visiting Hades or Hell to drop off all humankind's multitudinous load of sins, then their comma choice was correct. However, we know that Jesus did not yet have His Glorified Body based on what He said to Mary Magdalene on Sunday at the tomb.

John 20:17 Jesus saith unto her, Touch me not; for I am not yet ascended to my Father: but go to my brethren, and say unto them, I ascend unto my Father, and your Father; and to my God, and your God. (KJV)

Comma placement often totally changes the connotation or flavor of what was meant by a piece of text. In the statement made by Jesus to the repentant thief, did the translators make the right choice of comma-placement? Knowledgeable theologians have much debated their decision. Only God knows for sure. What do you think?

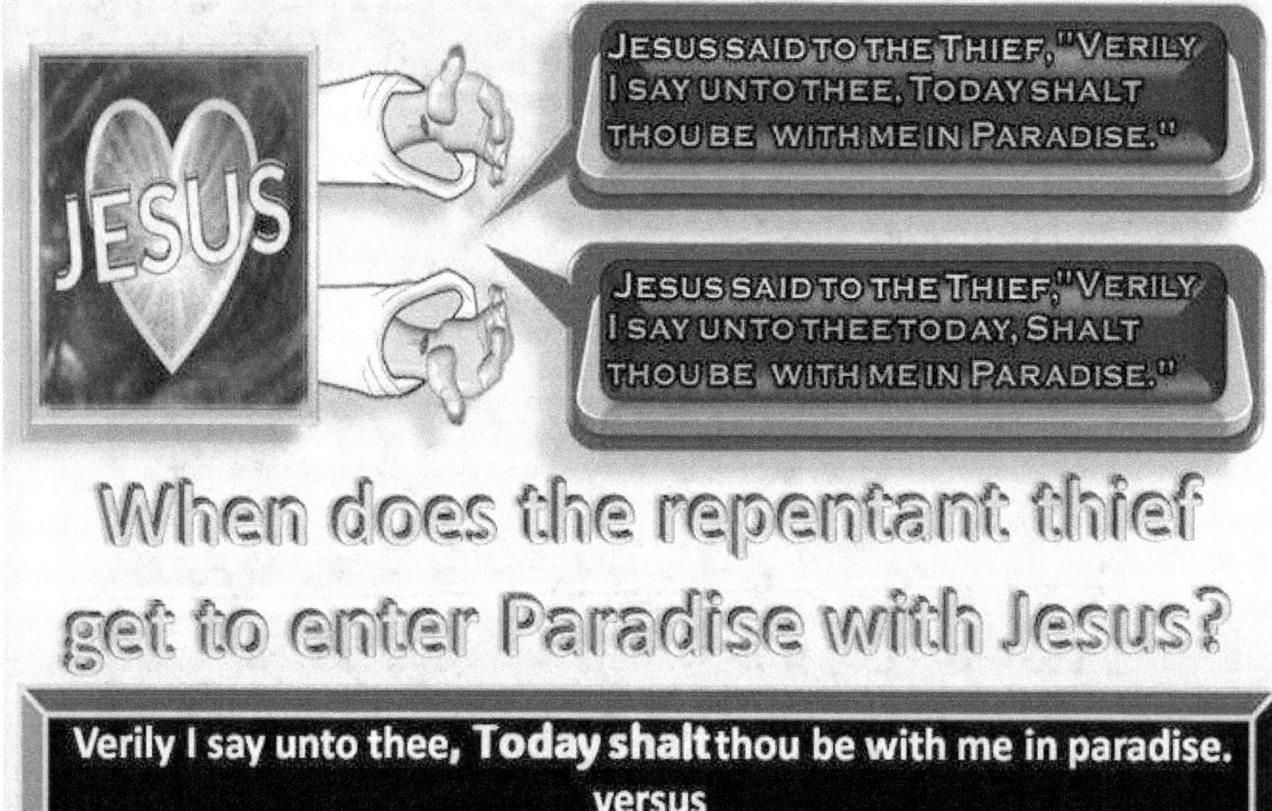

The contrite thief may have wondered something similar.

The other thief might have even made some cruel remarks to try to instill doubts in his former buddy.

The Holy Spirit would have continued speaking comfort and promissory joy to the contrite thief. He would reassure him that he now had the right to PLEAD THE BLOOD OF JESUS that would grant him entrance into Heaven. He just had to be patient a little longer.

The contrite thief was the first one to pray the Sinner's Prayer. Thanks to that, he won't suffer an eternity in hell. If you have not already accepted this free gift of Salvation, please don't delay. None of us are guaranteed tomorrow.

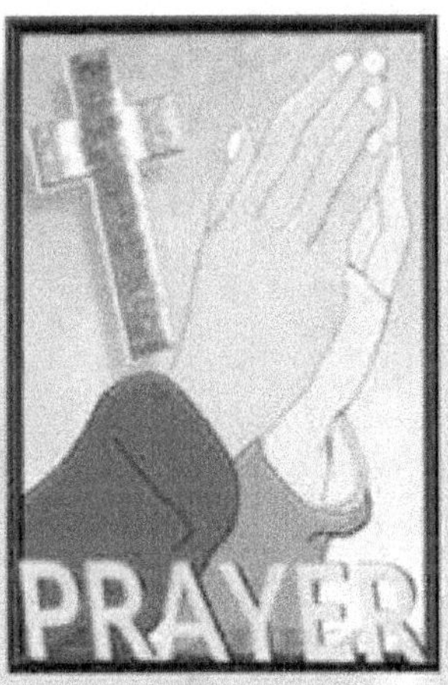

Dear Lord Jesus, I know that I am a sinner, and I ask for Your forgiveness. I believe You died for my sins and rose from the dead. I turn from my sins and invite You to come into my heart and life. I want to trust and follow You as my Lord and Savior. -- GOOGLE QUOTE

Crucifixion of Jesus Christ – our Savior & Lord

Examine 4 Gospels for Clues (KJV) — BIBLE CLUES (KJV)

Matthew, Mark, & Luke	John 19:25-27
No Reference to this Topic.	**25** Now there stood by the cross of Jesus his mother, and his mother's sister, Mary the wife of Cleophas, and Mary Magdalene. **26** When Jesus therefore saw his mother, and the disciple standing by, whom he loved, he saith unto his mother, Woman, behold thy son! **27** Then saith he to the disciple, Behold thy mother! And from that hour that disciple took her unto his own home.

Jesus had been hanging on the Cross for more than six hours. The time would soon come when He and the Father had pre-determined that He should conclude this earthly life. He was just minutes away from doing that very thing.

John 10:17 Therefore doth my Father love me, because I lay down my life, that I might take it again. **(KJV)**

18 No man taketh it from me, but I lay it down of myself. I have power to lay it down, and I have power to take it again. This commandment have I received of my Father.

Before He took His last breath, Jesus knew it was necessary to make provisions for His earthly mother. Yes, He had half-brothers who could take care of her physical needs, but He knew taking care of her spiritual needs was more vital. Above all other men, Jesus trusted His faithful Disciple John to do that very thing. In this way, it would comfort John and His beloved mother.

Jesus wanted to prevent as much of her suffering as He could. Unlike other children, Jesus had never thrown a tantrum or been rude to his mother. He had always been protective of her feelings. Nevertheless, her suffering was prophesied by Simeon when Jesus was but 40 days old. Listen to what had occurred on that long-ago day.

As described in **Luke 2:22-24**, forty days after Jesus' birth, Mary and her husband Joseph took baby Jesus to the Jerusalem temple to be dedicated.

We learn in **Luke 2:25-35** that there was an older man named Simeon. The Holy Ghost had promised this good man that he would not die until he had been allowed to see the *'Lord's Christ.'* (**Verse 26**)

So, on this particular day, the Holy Ghost directed Simeon to the temple.

Luke 2:28 Then took he him up in his arms, and blessed God, and said, 29 Lord, now lettest thou thy servant depart in peace, according to thy word: **30** For mine eyes have seen thy salvation, **31** Which thou hast prepared before the face of all people; **32** A light to lighten the Gentiles, and the glory of thy people Israel. **(KJV)**

Mary and Joseph were amazed at hearing this. Then, Simeon gave the following prophecy that must have given Mary a chilled feeling.

Luke 2:34 And Simeon blessed them, and said unto Mary his mother, Behold, this child is set for the fall and rising again of many in Israel; and for a sign which shall be spoken against; **35** (Yea, **a sword shall pierce through thy own soul** also,) that the thoughts of many hearts may be revealed. **(KJV)**

We learn in **Luke 2:36-38** that Mary and Joseph also encountered a widowed prophetess named Anna, who was likely 103 or older. How do we know this? We learn in **Luke 2:36** that she was a virgin of perhaps 12 to 14 years of age when she married. After seven years, she was widowed. She then spent the next 84 years serving in the temple. So, **84 + 7 + 12* = 103.** (or older) * *That number is dependent on the age she was when she married.*

Luke 2:37 And she was a widow of about fourscore and four years, which departed not from the temple, but served God with fastings and prayers night and day. **38 And she coming in that instant gave thanks likewise unto the Lord, and** spake of him to all them that looked for redemption in Jerusalem. **(KJV)**

Jesus knew that it was not only Jewish tradition to take care of and honor your parents, but it was also Biblical.

Exodus 20:12 Honour thy father and thy mother: that thy days may be long upon the land which the Lord thy God giveth thee. **(KJV)**

1 Timothy 5:8 But if any provide not for his own, and specially for those of his own house, he hath denied the faith, and is worse than an infidel. (KJV)

In the Old Testament, Moses was the first Prophet to predict the future birth and life of Jesus. Hosea, Micah, Jeremiah, and Isaiah also predicted His birth.

Genesis 3:15 And I will put enmity between thee and the woman, and between thy seed and her seed; it shall bruise thy head, and thou shalt bruise his heel. (KJV)

Genesis 49:10 The scepter shall not depart from Judah, nor a lawgiver from between his feet, until Shiloh come; and unto him shall the gathering of the people be. (KJV)

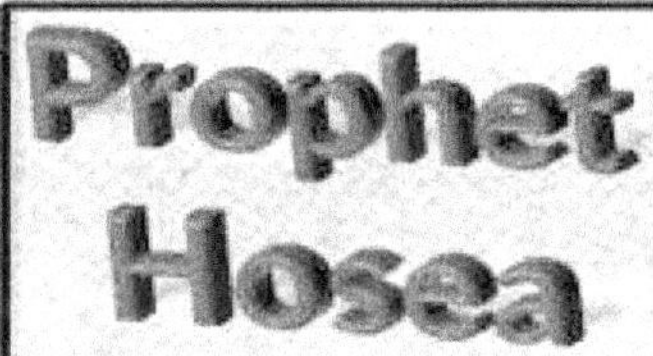

Hosea 11:1 When Israel was a child, then I loved him, and called my son out of Egypt. (KJV)

[FYI – This was a foreshadowing of part of Jesus' life.]

You may recall, from **Matthew 2:13-18**, that Mary, Joseph, and baby Jesus had to escape to Egypt to prevent Jesus from being killed along with all other male babies and toddlers in Bethlehem. Once Herod died, who had issued that cruel proclamation, Joseph, Mary, and Jesus could return and make their home in Nazareth. Why did Joseph and Mary go to Bethlehem in the first place? In **Luke 2:4-7**, we learn that since both Joseph and Mary were of the house and lineage of King David, they had to go to Bethlehem to be taxed.

Micah 5:2 But thou, Bethlehem Ephratah, though thou be little among the thousands of Judah, yet out of thee shall he come forth unto me that is to be ruler in Israel; whose goings forth have been from of old, from everlasting. (KJV)

Jeremiah 23:5 Behold, the days come, saith the Lord, that I will raise unto David a righteous Branch, and a King shall reign and prosper, and shall execute judgment and justice in the earth. (KJV)

Isaiah 7:14 Therefore the Lord himself shall give you a sign; Behold, a virgin shall conceive, and bear a son, and shall call his name Immanuel. (KJV)

FYI - Immanuel or Emmanuel means "God is with us."

Here is one last very familiar-sounding prophecy about Jesus given by Isaiah.

Isaiah 9:6 **For unto us a child is born, unto us a son is given**: and the government shall be upon his shoulder: and his name shall be called Wonderful, Counsellor, The mighty God, The everlasting Father, The Prince of Peace. (KJV)

Prince of Peace

Isaiah 9:7 Of the increase of his government and peace there shall be no end, upon the **throne of David**, and upon his kingdom, to order it, and to establish it with judgment and with justice from henceforth even for ever. The zeal of the Lord of hosts will perform this.

Jesus looked down Lovingly at two of His favorite people. He mustered some of His last remaining strength to say:

Jesus still had two more statements to say. To speak, He needed to gather just a little saliva to wet His dry, parched, dehydrated system. So, He gasped out the words, "I thirst." By doing so, He also fulfilled another Prophecy.

Crucifixion of Jesus Christ – our Savior & Lord

BIBLE CLUES ??? (KJV) Examine 4 Gospels for Clues (KJV) ??? BIBLE CLUES (KJV)	
Matthew, Mark, & Luke	**John 19:28-29**
Matthew & Mark details that Jesus refused the offer of vinegar at the onset of the crucifixion. **Luke makes no reference to this topic.**	**28** After this, Jesus knowing that all things were now accomplished, that the scripture might be fulfilled, saith, I thirst. **29** Now there was set a vessel full of vinegar: and they filled a spunge with vinegar, and put it upon hyssop, and put it to his mouth.

We learn in **Matthew 27:48** and **Mark 15:36** that after Jesus gasped out His statement about being thirsty, one of the Roman soldiers took pity on Jesus. This soldier ran, filled a sponge with vinegar, attached that sponge to a reed long enough to reach Jesus' lips, and gave Him a drink.

Matthew 27:48 And straightway one of them ran, and took a spunge, and filled it with vinegar, and put it on a reed, and gave him to drink. (KJV)

Mark 15:36 And one ran and filled a spunge full of vinegar, and put it on a reed, and gave him to drink, … (KJV)

Notice, in **John 19:26**, John stated: "They filled a sponge with vinegar, and put it upon HYSSOP, and put it to his mouth."

Psalm 51:7 Purge me with hyssop, and I shall be clean: wash me, and I shall be whiter than snow.
(Verse 8 not applicable to this point.)

Psalm 51:9 Hide thy face from my sins, and blot out all mine iniquities.

Psalm 51:10 Create in me a clean heart, O God; and renew a right spirit within me.

Psalm 51:11 Cast me not away from thy presence; and take not thy holy spirit from me.

Psalm 51:12 Restore unto me the joy of thy salvation; and uphold me with thy free spirit. (KJV)

"What hyssop represents, especially in Psalm 51, still applies to every believer. We are by nature sinful and cannot fix ourselves. But David's words show us we don't have to stay stuck in that place. If we admit our need for God's touch and humbly ask Him to forgive us, He will bring a deep cleansing.

And in this age, we receive that renewal in a different way. Instead of going to a priest to be sprinkled with the blood of an animal, we put our faith in Jesus. Christ shed His blood on the cross so that we could be made righteous before God."

You may be wondering why King David needed to be cleansed by HYSSOP. We learn in **2 Samuel 12:1-8** that God sent Prophet Nathan to confront David about sinning with the beautiful Bathsheba and accidentally getting her pregnant. Then, to cover up their adulterous affair, he had her husband, Uriah, killed in battle. The prophet said the following:

2 Samuel 12:9 Wherefore hast thou despised the commandment of the Lord, to do evil in his sight? thou hast killed Uriah the Hittite with the sword, and hast taken his wife to be thy wife, and hast slain him with the sword of the children of Ammon. **(KJV)**

We learn, in **2 Samuel 12:15-23**, that their first child died. It must have been during this period that David begged the Lord to wash him clean with HYSSOP.

In **2 Samuel 12:24**, we also discover that their second child was the future King Solomon. Jesus' mother, Mary, was a direct descendant of the second child of David and Bathsheba. *SEE THE FAMILY TREE ON UPCOMING PAGE.*

As you will see on the next page, the fifth living child of King David and Bathsheba was **Nathan**. Nathan was the direct ancestor of **Joseph, the foster father of Jesus**. How do I know that to be true? Please read the fascinating article found on their website, *Conforming to Jesus.com*. For your convenience, I have listed this article in the Bibliography. The one I found most enlightening was "Why are Jesus' Genealogies in Matthew and Luke different?"

In short, this is what I learned.

Nathan's line leads to the foster father, Joseph, whereas King Solomon's line leads to the Virgin Mary.

When reading the first chapter of the Book of Matthew, please observe **Matthew 1:1-16** describes the lineage that begins with Abraham, Isaac, Jacob, his fourth-born son, Judas (aka Judah), …, Booz (aka Boaz), Obed, Jesse, King David, **Solomon**, …, Joseph, Mary, Jesus Christ.

Allegedly, there was a translation error. It should have read father of Mary — not husband of Mary.

the father of Mary,

Matthew 1:16 And Jacob begat Joseph, the husband of Mary, of whom was born Jesus, who is called Christ.

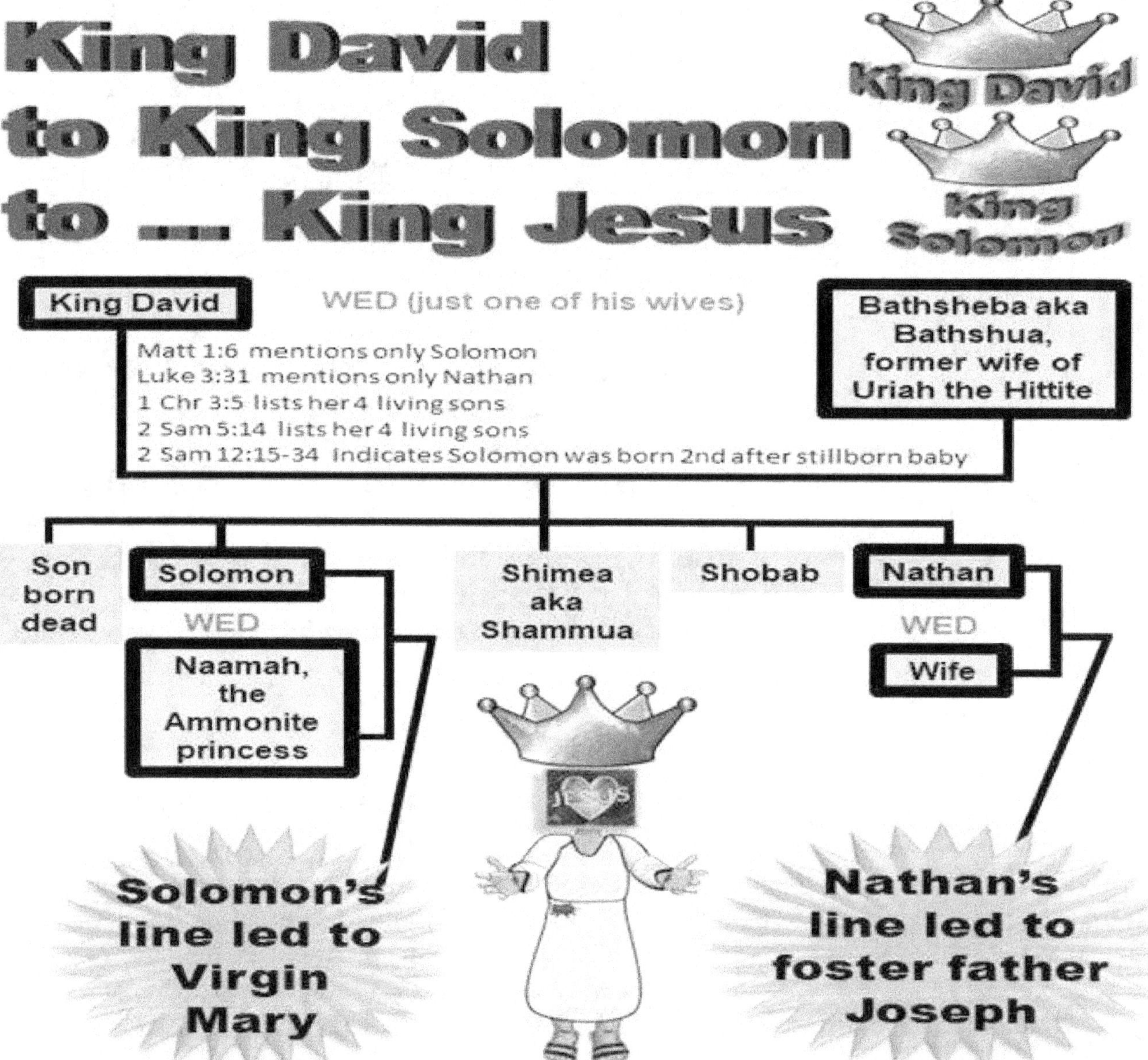

So, the Virgin Mary had a father named Joseph and a husband with the widespread first name of Joseph.

On the other hand, Luke's genealogy found in **Luke 3:23-38** starts with Jesus, who was supposed to be the son of **Joseph**, who was the son of Heli. He continues with this line through Nathan, who was the son of David, who was the son of Jesse, who was the son of Obed, who was the son of Booz (aka Boaz), …, who was the son of Juda (aka Judas aka Judah), who was the son of Jacob, who was the son of Isaac, who was the son of Abraham, …, who was the son of Noe (aka Noah), …, who was the son of Seth, who was the son of Adam, which was the son of God.

Nathan's line followed the lineage of His foster father, Joseph, to demonstrate that he was a fitting husband for the Virgin Mary. In that way, both parents (foster father Joseph and biological mother Mary) would raise Jesus in a God-fearing home.

So, Matthew follows the line of King David's son, Solomon. **Luke follows the line of King David's son, Nathan.**

FYI – Matthew 1:16 reads that Joseph was her husband and Jacob was her father. That article shows Jacob was her grandfather instead.

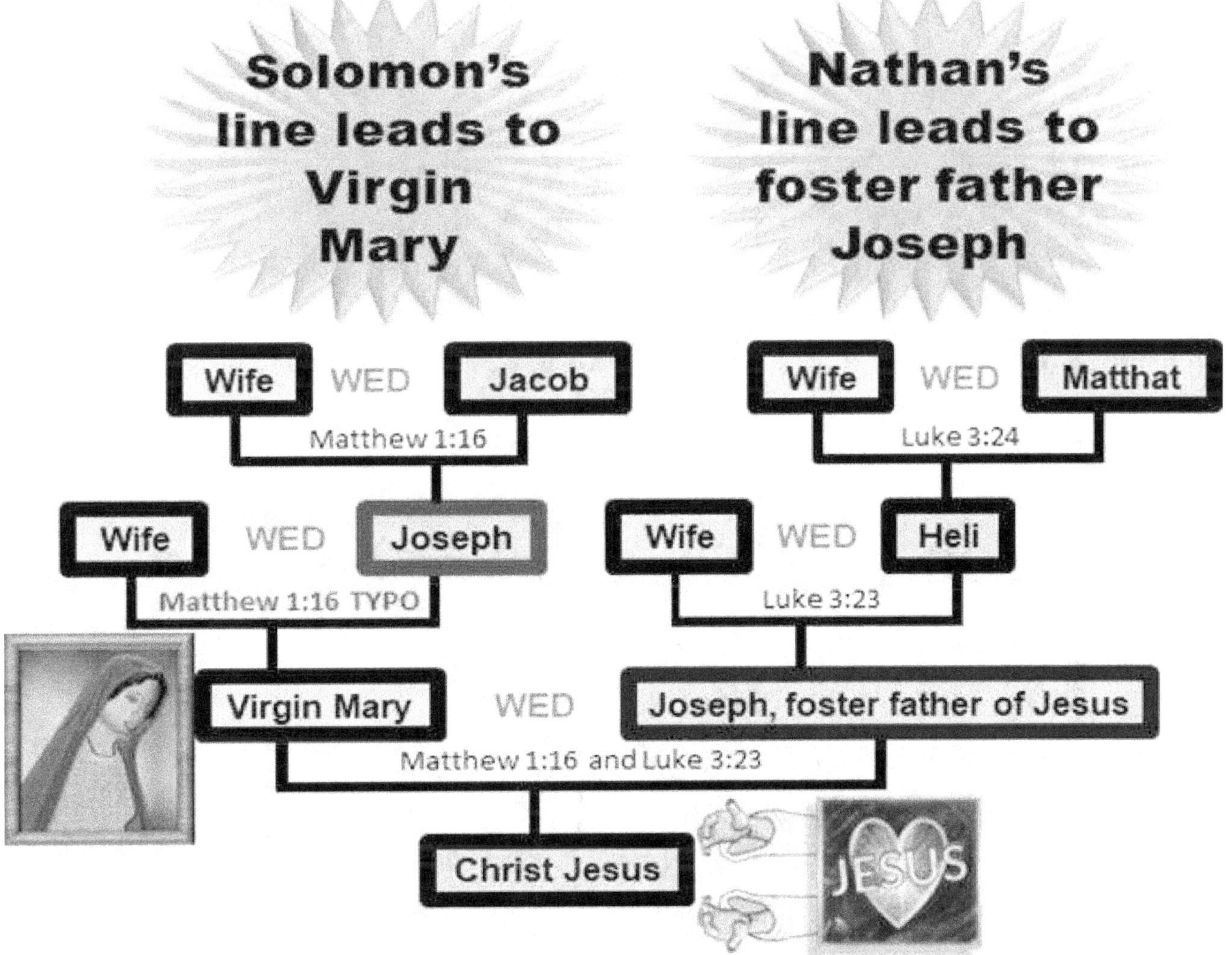

Here are some other intriguing facts about Hyssop in the Bible.

In **Exodus 12:21-25**, we learn God directed Moses to tell the Jews to use HYSSOP to keep them safe when all the firstborns in Egypt were going to die.

> **Exodus 12:21** Then Moses summoned all the elders of Israel and said to them, "Go at once and select the animals for your families and slaughter the Passover lamb.
>
> **Exodus 12:22** Take a bunch of hyssop, dip it into the blood in the basin and put some of the blood on the top and on both sides of the doorframe. None of you shall go out of the door of your house until morning.
>
> **Exodus 12:23** When the Lord goes through the land to strike down the Egyptians, he will see the blood on the top and sides of the doorframe and will pass over that doorway, and he will not permit the destroyer to enter your houses and strike you down.
>
> **Exodus 12:24** Obey these instructions as a lasting ordinance for you and your descendants.
>
> **Exodus 12:25** When you enter the land that the Lord will give you as he promised, observe this ceremony. (NIV)

Numbers 19:17-20 (NIV) described a final example of how the Children of Israel used **HYSSOP** for cleansing.

> **Numbers 19:17 For the unclean person, put some ashes from the burned purification offering into a jar and pour fresh water over them.**
>
> **Numbers 19:18 Then a man who is ceremonially clean is to take some hyssop, dip it in the water and sprinkle the tent and all the furnishings and the people who were there. He must also sprinkle anyone who has touched a human bone or a grave or anyone who has been killed or anyone who has died a natural death.**
>
> **Numbers 19:19 The man who is clean is to sprinkle those who are unclean on the third and seventh days, and on the seventh day he is to purify them. Those who are being cleansed must wash their clothes and bathe with water, and that evening they will be clean.**
>
> **Numbers 19:20 But if those who are unclean do not purify themselves, they must be cut off from the community, because they have defiled the sanctuary of the Lord. The water of cleansing has not been sprinkled on them, and they are unclean. (NIV)**

So, let's return to Jesus on the Cross, who announced, "I thirst." We know a Roman soldier ran and filled a sponge with vinegar, attached it to a **HYSSOP** reed, and lifted this to Jesus' mouth so He could drink.

I heard a preacher suggest that the vinegar only wet Jesus' lips; nevertheless, it provided Him just enough saliva to utter His final two statements.

In any case, I was relieved to see that at least one Roman soldier felt enough compassion that he at least tried to give Jesus a little relief.

When I watched movies about the crucifixion and heard Jesus cry out, "I thirst," I often found myself thinking about what Jesus said to the Samaritan woman at the well. I would spend some moments speculating why Jesus could not access that 'living water' he told her about. Then, I would remind myself that nothing comforting could happen to Him in those moments; otherwise, the Scriptures would not be fulfilled.

Here is a shortened reminder of the story about Jesus' encounter with the Samaritan woman, written in **John 4:1-42**.

Jesus and His Disciples took a shortcut through Samaria to get from Judea to Galilee. To do this was shocking to both His Disciples and the Samaritans, as back then, Jews did not have anything to do with Samaritans.

Father God directed His Son to do this as He wanted Jesus to meet up with a Samaritan woman who had already been married five times and was living with a man outside of marriage at their encounter. Due to the life she led, she was not welcome to draw water at **'Jacob's Well'** with the other women. Instead, she had to go there by herself at noon each day.

While the Disciples had gone into town for provisions, Jesus respectfully asked the Samaritan woman for a drink of water. She could not understand why He would ask such a thing of her since she had never heard of any Jew willingly having anything to do with Samaritans.

In **John 4:10**, Jesus said, "If you knew the gift of God and who it is that asks you for a drink, you would have asked him, and he would have given you living water."

In **John 4:11-12**, the Samaritan woman said, "Sir, you have nothing to draw with, and the well is deep. Where can you get this living water? Are you greater than our father Jacob, who gave us the well and drank from it himself, as did also his sons and his livestock?"

In **John 4:13-14**, Jesus said, "Everyone who drinks this water will be thirsty again, but whoever drinks the water I give them will never thirst. Indeed, the water I give them will become in them a spring of water welling up to eternal life."

The woman was excited and amazed. In **John 4:15**, she asked, "Sir, give me this water so that I won't get thirsty and have to keep coming here to draw water."

That was when Jesus revealed He knew her circumstances. She was impressed and said, in **John 4:19**, "Sir, I perceive that You are a prophet. **20** Our fathers worshipped on this mountain, and you *Jews* say that in Jerusalem is the place where one ought to worship."

In **John 4:21**, Jesus said to her, "Woman, believe Me, the hour is coming when you will neither on this mountain, nor in Jerusalem, worship the Father. **22** You worship what you do not know; we know what we worship, for salvation is of the Jews. **23** But the hour is coming, and now is, when the true worshippers will worship the Father in spirit and truth; for the Father is seeking such to worship Him. **24** God *is* Spirit, and those who worship Him must worship in spirit and truth."

In **John 4:25**, the woman said to Jesus, "I know that Messiah is coming" (who is called Christ). "When He comes, He will tell us all things."

In **John 4:26**, Jesus told her, "I who speak to you am *He.*"

The Samaritan woman was so excited that she ran into town, telling everyone what occurred. Everyone was impressed and excited when they heard her say, in **John 4:29**, "Come, see a man, which told me all things that ever I did: is not this the Christ?"

Jesus spent two days with her people who believed and stated, in **John 4:42**, "Now we believe, not because of thy saying: for we have heard him ourselves, and know that this is indeed the Christ, the Savior of the world."

So, the Samaritan people believed Jesus was the Messiah long before His people did.

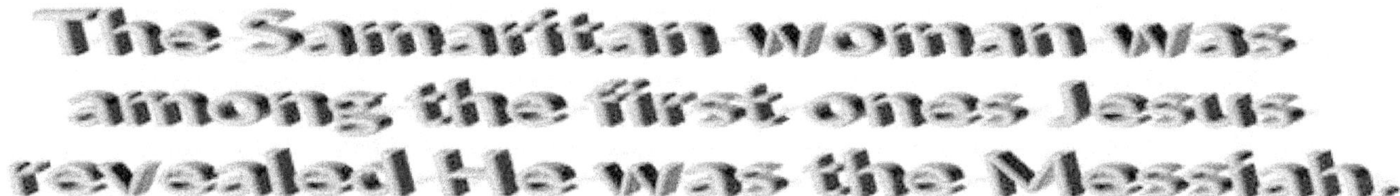

As I reflect further about Jesus' struggles with thirst while on the Cross, perhaps that, too, could be of comfort to those of us in the flesh who suffer from thirsts of various types:

- **Water**
- **Juices**
- **Soft Drinks**
- **Caffeinated Drinks**
- **Coffee**
- **Tea (Hot or Iced)**
- **Beer and other types of Alcohol**
- **OR thirst for possessions such as followers, receiving a certain number of likes, owning a certain number of cars, houses, designer items such as purses, shoes, clothes, etc., or experiencing the status of being rich.**
- **Or thirst for the experience of being popular, famous, admired, loved, wise, talented, skilled, strong, beautiful, handsome, closer to God, filled with the Holy Spirit, seeing Jesus face-to-face, etc.**

Because Jesus understands what it means to suffer from thirst, we can feel fellowship with Him when we, too, are thirsting. Here is a suggested prayer:

To recap, after hanging on the cross for six hours (9 AM to 3 PM), Jesus finally had seven (7) things to say. He had two explicit purposes for making the statement: "**I Thirst.**" Firstly, it was a **REMEZ** pointing back to King David's Psalm 22:15 and Psalm 69:21 prophecies. Secondly, Jesus needed to get together just enough saliva so that He was able to utter three final Remez-laden remarks.

See next page

FYI – Jesus needed to wet His mouth so He could utter His final statements before dying.

Crucifixion of Jesus Christ – our Savior & Lord

Examine 4 Gospels for Clues (KJV)

Matthew 27:46-50	Mark 15:34-37	Luke & John
46 And about the ninth hour Jesus cried with a loud voice, saying, **Eli, Eli, lama sabachthani?** that is to say, **My God, my God, why hast thou forsaken me?**	34 And at the ninth hour Jesus cried with a loud voice, saying, **Eloi, Eloi, lama sabachthani?** which is, being interpreted, **My God, my God, why hast thou forsaken me?**	No Reference to this Topic.
47 Some of them that stood there, when they heard that, said, **This man calleth for Elias (i.e., Isaiah).**	35 And some of them that stood by, when they heard it, said, **Behold, he calleth Elias (i.e., Isaiah).**	
48 And straightway one of them ran, and took a spunge, and filled it with vinegar, and put it on a reed, and gave him to drink.	36 And one ran and filled a spunge full of vinegar, and put it on a reed, and gave him to drink, saying, **Let alone; let us see whether Elias will come to take him down.**	
49 The rest said, **Let be, let us see whether Elias will come to save him.**		
50 Jesus, when he had cried again with a loud voice, yielded up the ghost.	37 And Jesus cried with a loud voice, and gave up the ghost.	

In **Matthew 27:47-49** and **Mark 15:35-36**, the Jews thought they heard Jesus calling for Elias, aka Isaiah, an Old Testament Prophet. Below is some information about this prophet.

I am not the only one who has found Jesus crying out these words (i.e., "My God, my God, why hast thou forsaken me?") particularly distressing. I have often questioned what the intention was behind His words.

Here is Remez's hidden message, taken from King David's **Psalm 22:1-3**.

REMEZ – Hidden Messages

Psalm 22:1 My God, my God, why hast thou forsaken me? why art thou so far from helping me, and from the words of my roaring? (KJV)

Psalm 22:2 O my God, I cry in the day time, but thou hearest not; and in the night season, and am not silent. (KJV)

Psalm 22:3 But thou art holy, O thou that inhabitest the praises of Israel. (KJV)

In Wikipedia, I found these three different interpretations. The first one definitely would illicit the educated Jews back in His day to think of King David crying out the very same words.

REMEZ – Hidden Messages

King David — prophesied & foreshadowed

From Wikipedia:
"Sayings of Jesus on the cross"

"Others see these words in the context of Psalm 22 and suggest that Jesus recited these words, perhaps even the whole psalm, 'that he might show himself to be the very Being to whom the words refer; so that the Jewish scribes and people might examine and see the cause why he would not descend from the cross; namely, because this very psalm showed that it was appointed that he should suffer these things.'"

This second explanation makes a lot of sense. After all, in those moments on the cross and the thirty-three years that had passed, Jesus was fully human. As a human, He likely felt forsaken, abandoned, and deserted. I wonder if He might have briefly entertained the idea of the angels swooping in to save Him without being asked.

This explanation would also be appropriate for all who are fully human. We would be aware that when we feel similar emotions; Jesus would know how we feel. That might bring people some moments of comfort.

"This saying is taken by some as an abandonment of the Son by the Father."

"Other theologians understand the cry as that of one who was truly human and who felt forsaken. Put to death by his foes, very largely deserted by his friends, he may have also felt deserted by God.'"

Here is the final interpretation from Wikipedia. This explanation matches the theory I have often heard preached on Easter Sunday.

Crucifixion of Jesus Christ – our Savior & Lord

BIBLE CLUES ??? (KJV) Examine 4 Gospels for Clues (KJV) ??? BIBLE CLUES (KJV)

Matthew 27:50	Mark 15:37	Luke 23:46	John
50 Jesus, when he had cried again with a loud voice, yielded up the ghost.	**37** And Jesus cried with a loud voice, and gave up the ghost.	**46** And when Jesus had cried with a loud voice, he said, **Father, into thy hands I commend my spirit** and having said thus, he gave up the ghost.	No Reference to this Topic.

Here is the Remez Hidden Message for Jesus' words from the Cross: "Father, into thy hands I commend my spirit."

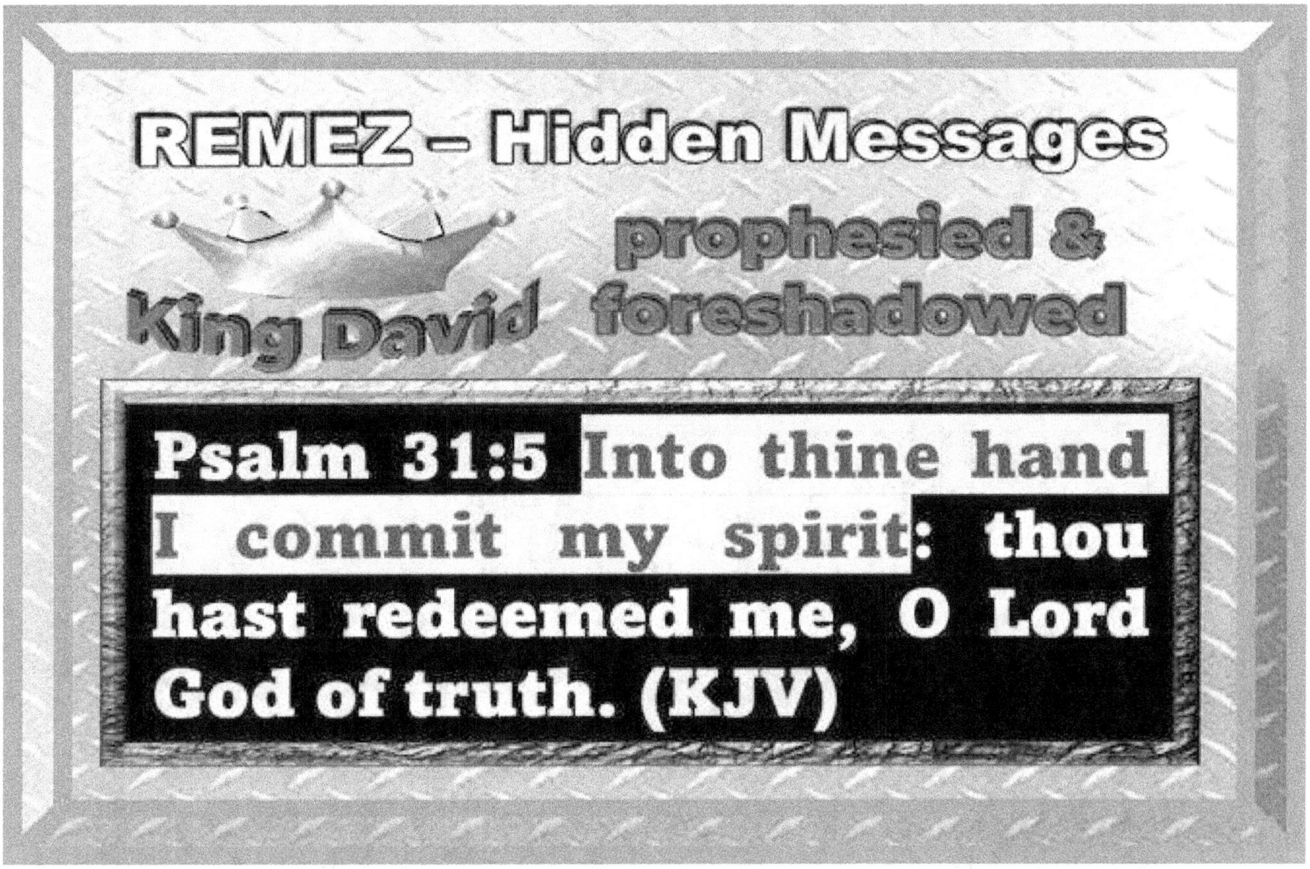

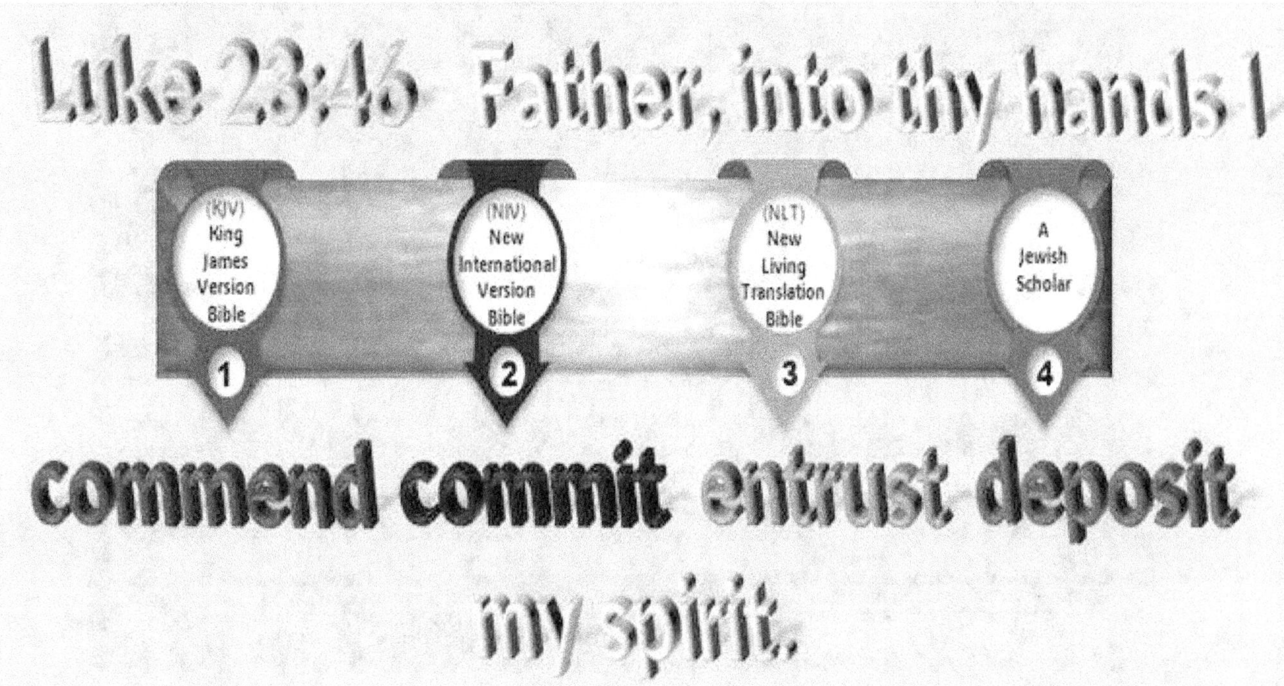

Using Bible Hub, here are four connotations on the word Jesus used from the Cross: "Father, into thy hand I [____] my spirit." [commend, commit, entrust, deposit]

I found it fascinating to learn that King David's statement, pulled from **Psalm 31:5**, has been used by multiple Jews for centuries as part of their evening prayer. This practice likely included the Sanhedrin, Jesus, and His Disciples.

"The Jewish morning begins with the "Modeh Ani" ("I thank") prayer, which expresses the worshiper's gratitude towards the Heavenly King for returning one's soul to him or her. The presumption here is that the evening before the worshiper has entrusted the spirit to the Almighty for safe-keeping. Many observant Jews use the phrase in "Into your hands I commit my spirit" (Psalm 31:5) at the end of their evening prayers.

The Hebrew word which was translated as "I commit" is "אַפְקִיד" (pronounced afkid). This word has a meaning that is much closer to "I deposit" – which necessarily signifies a future "reclaiming" of the thing deposited. ... In Hebrew, on the other hand, the unequivocal meaning of this verse is the temporary submission of one's spirit into the hands of God, into "His custody", with the definite intention of receiving it back."

Luke 8:55 **And her spirit came again, and she arose straightway: and he commanded to give her meat.** (KJV)

Job 33:4 **The spirit of God hath made me, and the breath of the Almighty hath given me life.** (KJV)

FYI –
Luke 8:40-42, 49-56 – Jairus' 12-year-old daughter died. Jesus brought her back to life.

SPIRIT

Ecclesiastes 12:7 **Then shall the dust return to the earth as it was: and the spirit shall return unto God who gave it.** (KJV)

James 2:26 **For as the body without the spirit is dead, so faith without works is dead also.** (KJV)

Crucifixion of Jesus Christ – our Savior & Lord

Examine 4 Gospels for Clues (KJV)

 Matthew 27:50	Mark 15:37	Luke 23:46	John 19:30
50 Jesus, when he had cried again with a loud voice, yielded up the ghost.	**37** And Jesus cried with a loud voice, and gave up the ghost.	**46** … and having said thus, he gave up the ghost.	**30** When Jesus therefore had received the vinegar, he said, It is finished: and he bowed his head, and gave up the ghost.

Using Bible Hub, here are four connotations for how the Gospels describe Jesus' final moments of life.

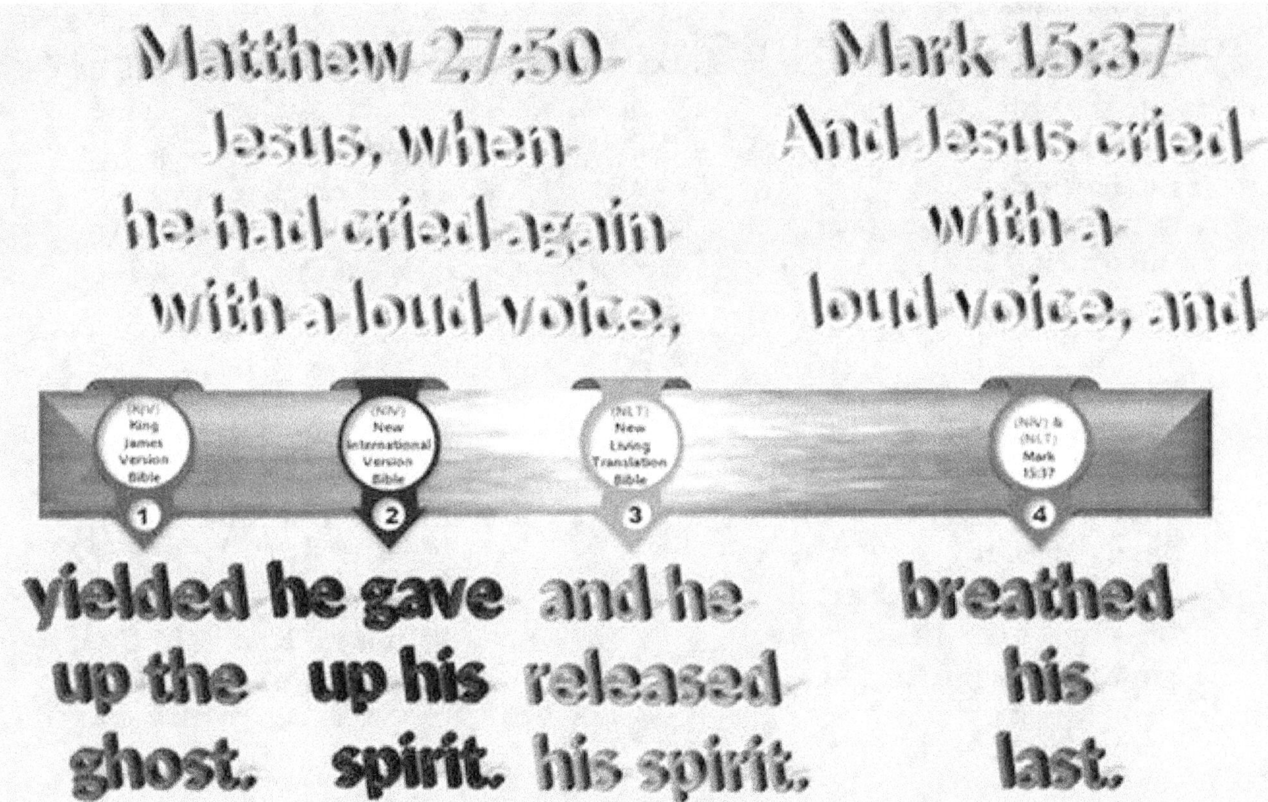

Here is another explanation about the timing of Jesus' death on the Cross.

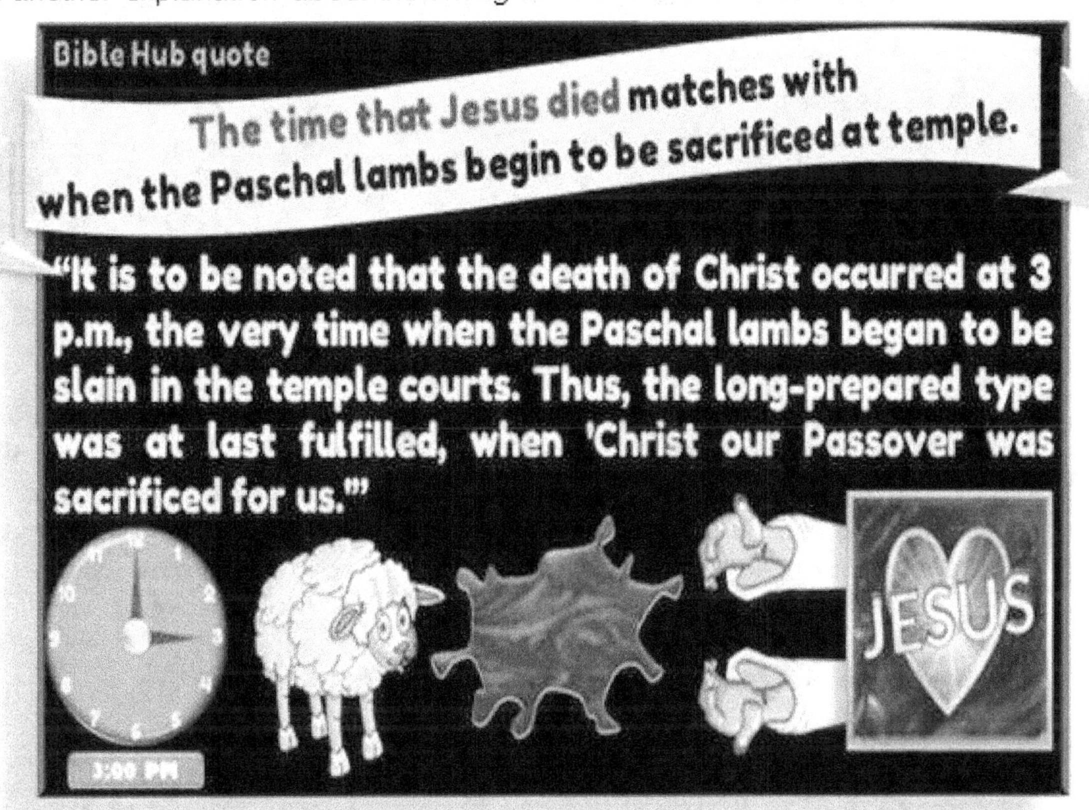

Since it is unclear which statement was Jesus' final statement, here is one final recap with its correlating Remez statement that includes them both.

REMEZ – Hidden Messages

Matthew 27:50 And when Jesus had cried out again in a loud voice, he gave up his spirit. (NIV)

Mark 15:37 With a loud cry, Jesus breathed his last. (NIV)

John 19:30 When he had received the drink, Jesus said, "It is finished." With that, he bowed his head and gave up his spirit. (NIV)

Luke 23:46 Jesus called out with a loud voice, "Father, into your hands I commit my spirit." When he had said this, he breathed his last. (NIV)

Psalm 22:31 They will come and declare His righteousness To a people yet to be born—that He has done it [and that it is finished]. (Amplified Bible)

Psalm 31:5 Into your hands I commit my spirit; deliver me, Lord, my faithful God. (NIV)

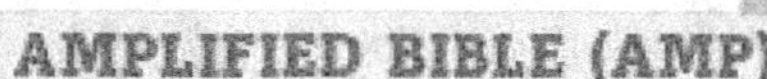

AMPLIFIED BIBLE (AMP)

Psalm 22:27 All the ends of the earth will remember and turn to the Lord, And all the families of the nations will bow down and worship before You, **28** For the kingship and the kingdom are the Lord's And He rules over the nations. **29** All the prosperous of the earth will eat and worship; All those who go down to the dust (the dead) will bow before Him, Even he who cannot keep his soul alive. **30** Posterity will serve Him; They will tell of the Lord to the next generation.

Psalm 22:31 They will come and declare His righteousness To a people yet to be born—that He has done it [and that it is finished].

1. How long was Jesus silent on the Cross before speaking?

2. How many statements did Jesus speak from the Cross?

3. What do you now understand about Jesus' first statement from the Cross about forgiveness?

4. What do you now understand about Jesus' second statement from the Cross about one of the thieves?

5. What do you now understand about Jesus' third statement from the Cross about what Jesus said to His mother and Disciple John?

6. What do you now understand about Jesus' fourth statement from the Cross about being thirsty?

7. What do you now understand about Jesus' fifth statement from the Cross about feeling forsaken?

8. What do you now understand about Jesus' sixth statement from the Cross about commending or committing His Spirit?

9. What do you now understand about Jesus' seventh and final statement from the Cross about it was now finished?

10. What other thoughts do you have to share about Jesus' six hours on the Cross?

11. 

Role-play: Act it out or Journal about it.

Possible Actors: Jesus, 2 Thieves, Roman Soldiers, and Pharisees

Plot: Act out or journal about the interaction between Jesus, the angry thief, and the repentant thief. You might want to add in possible statements made by either the Roman soldiers or Pharisees reacting to what Jesus said to the repentant thief.

Author's Dedication

There are many ways to demonstrate our love for and worship of our Lord Jesus Christ. This book is a rendering of data points for you to prayerfully consider that might give your worship of Him a deeper dimension. I dedicate this book to all honest seekers of truth. May it provide another viewing point of the **WORD** in the Holy Bible.

Author's Acknowledgements

There was a deeper purpose for authoring this book. I wrote this book not for my glory but for the glory of our Heavenly God the Father, God the Son, and God the Holy Spirit. I am so grateful for all the manifold ways God, the **Trinity of three Persons**, continually blesses my life. May this book bless your life, as well.

I acknowledge and am so grateful for all the people who created the Bible APPS, Google, Microsoft PowerPoint, Microsoft Word, the Paint APP, books, videos, movies, talks, and sermons that fed my imagination and blessed my life. I also acknowledge the countless moments of comfort and blessings I receive from my dear and treasured family and friends (both living and deceased), of which I count you, my readers, among them. I am eternally grateful! God bless you all! May you have a blessed and touched-by-God life!

Final Blessings

I find myself speculating if God planted me exactly where He did and gave me all the experiences that He gave me just so I could write this book.

And then I feel the **Holy Spirit** nudging me, reminding me of this Bible verse:

Romans 8:28 And we know that all things work together for good to them that love God, to them who are called according to his purpose. (KJV)

May the **Holy Spirit** touch and bless you, as well, and help you to fulfill the mission that God has prescribed just for you.

I end this book with two final blessings, one by King David, the other by Moses.

Psalm 121:8 The Lord keeps watch over you as you come and go, both now and forever. (NLT)

Numbers 6:24 The LORD bless you and keep you. 25 The LORD make his face shine upon you and be gracious to you. 26 The LORD turn his face toward you and give you peace. (NIV)

AMEN. Thank you for making the time to read a part or all of this book. Kindly consider leaving a review, even if it is only a sentence or two.

Also, if you found it pleasing, please share this book with the people you love.

BIBLIOGRAPHY

Bibliography: Used for entire book

Bible Gateway.com. (October 2023 to May 2024). Read the Bible. Website; https://www.biblegateway.com/

Developer Unknown. (October 2023 to May 2024). Bible – Daily Bible Verse KJV. From a free cell phone APP.

Google.com Search Engine. (October 2023 to May 2024).

Grammarly.com for editing (October 2023 to May 2024).

Kairos Software LLC. Developer. (October 2023 to May 2024). Bible KJV Strong's Concordance. From a free cell phone APP. (October – November 2023)

On-line dictionary via Google Search Engine. (October 2023 to May 2024).

Bibliography: Resources to increase my understanding

Abbott, Shari for Reasons for Hope * Jesus. (January 2024). Did Pilate Proclaim Jesus to be God? A Remez on the Cross. Website: https://reasonsforhopejesus.com/pilate-proclaimed-jesus-god/

Adams, Heather for Bible Study Tools.com. (November 2023). What Is Hyssop and Why Is It so Significant in the Bible? Website: https://www.biblestudytools.com/bible-study/topical-studies/what-is-hyssop-and-why-is-it-so-significant-in-the-bible.html

Bible Ask.org. (November 2023). What are the seven wounds or scars of Christ? Website: https://bibleask.org/what-are-the-seven-wounds-or-scars-of-christ/

Bible info.com. (March 2024). The thief on the cross, the comma & Christ. Website: https://www.bibleinfo.com/en/questions/thief-on-cross

Bible info.com. (February 2024). What time of day did the crucifixion happen? Website: https://www.bibleinfo.com/en/questions/what-time-day-did-crucifixion-happen

Bible Outlines.com. (January 2024). Luke 22:35-38 — Be Prepared for Suffering and Rejection. Website: https://www.bibleoutlines.com/luke-2235-38-be-prepared-for-suffering-and-rejection/

Bible questions.org. (April 2024). What does "kick against the pricks" mean? Website: https://www.biblequestions.org/bqar075.html

Colton, John for Frog.org. (January 2024). Did Pilate Proclaim Jesus to be God as Well as King of the Jews? Website: https://www.frog.org.nz/johns-blog/179

Conforming to Jesus Ministry.com. (June 2023). Why are Jesus' Genealogies in Matthew and Luke different? Website: https://www.conformingtojesus.com/why_are_jesus_genealogies_in_gospels_different.htm

Deep Believer with Jim Staley. (April 2024). 7 Wild Things Happening On April 8th PLUS It's Prophetic Solar Eclipse! Website: https://youtu.be/MBthvjsRDGU?si=4YonG9l4vqGEX-9v

Free Messianic Bible.com. (January 2024). The Controversy Over the Name of Yeshua. Website: https://free.messianicbible.com/feature/the-controversy-over-the-name-of-yeshua/

Got Questions.org. (January 2024). What time was Jesus crucified? Website: https://www.gotquestions.org/what-time-was-Jesus-crucified.html

Got Questions.org. (November 2023). Where do the Hebrew Scriptures prophesy the death and resurrection of the Messiah? Website: https://www.gotquestions.org/death-resurrection-Messiah.html

Hallingstad, Judy or Steps to Life.org. (April 2024). Question & Answer – Explain what is meant by "kick against the pricks" in Acts 9:5. Website: https://www.stepstolife.org/article/question-answer-explain-what-is-meant-by-kick-against-the-pricks-in-acts-95/

Henrickson, Rev. Charles. (December 2023). "Not One of His Bones Will Be Broken" (John 19:31-37). Website: https://stmatthewbt.org/2016/03/25/not-one-of-his-bones-will-be-broken-john-1931-37/

Lizorkin-Eyzenberg, Dr. Eli. (March 2024). Rethinking Jesus' words from the Hebrew original. Website: https://news.kehila.org/rethinking-jesus-words-from-from-the-hebrew-original/

Lizorkin-Eyzenberg, Dr. Eliyahu. (January 2024). The Hidden Hebrew Message on the Pilate's Cross. Website: https://weekly.israelbiblecenter.com/hidden-hebrew-message-pilates-cross

Missler, Chuck on YouTube. (January 2024). The Crucifixion of Jesus Christ - Dr. Chuck Missler. Website: https://www.youtube.com/watch?v=SLpXZKmhlHA

One for Israel.org. (November 2023). The Untold Reason why Jewish People do not believe Jesus is the Messiah! Website: https://www.oneforisrael.org/bible-based-teaching-from-israel/the-untold-reason-why-jewish-people-do-not-believe-jesus-is-the-messiah/

Passion for Truth Ministries on YouTube. (April 2024). The Connection to Passover to Pentecost - Jim Staley. Website: https://youtu.be/1_1uj6EX1co?si=-ivCqj2clKJSdiSb

Pedrow, Debra. (November 2023). Jesus Shed His Blood 7 Times For You. Website: https://debrapedrow.com/2020/04/02/jesus-shed-his-blood-7-times-for-you/

Penelope.uchicago.edu. (March 2024). The Death of Jesus. Website: https://penelope.uchicago.edu/~grout/encyclopaedia_romana/calendar/jesus.html

Shirley, Steve. (November 2023). Can you describe Jesus' physical sufferings on His final day? Website: https://jesusalive.cc/jesus-sufferings-final-day/

Shrier, Cahleen, Ph.D. for apu.edu. (February 2024). The Science of the Crucifixion. Website: https://www.apu.edu/articles/the-science-of-the-crucifixion/

Sproul, R.C., (November 2023). The Crucifixion and Old Testament Prophecy. Website: https://www.ligonier.org/learn/articles/crucifixion-and-old-testament-prophecy

Understand Christianity.com. (February 2024). Chronology of Jesus' Life and Ministry. Website: https://www.understandchristianity.com/timelines/chronology-jesus-life-ministry/

Wikipedia.org. (March 2024). Judas Iscariot. Website: https://en.wikipedia.org/wiki/Judas_Iscariot

Wikipedia.org. (November 2023). Mary Magdalene. Website: https://en.wikipedia.org/wiki/Mary_Magdalene

Wikipedia.org. (November 2023). Sayings of Jesus on the cross. Website: https://en.wikipedia.org/wiki/Sayings_of_Jesus_on_the_cross

Wilson, Larry W. for Wake-up.org. (November 2023). The Mystery of Mary Magdalene. Website: https://wake-up.org/bible-characters/mary-magdalene-mystery.html

Winger, Mike on YouTube. (January 2024). Really Specific Prophecy Jesus Fulfilled on the Cross! Amazing! Website: https://www.youtube.com/watch?v=eq8oaOix3rs

Thank you!

Thank you for making the time to read a part or all of this book.

Please leave a review.

Kindly consider leaving a review, even if it is only a sentence or two.

Share this with your loved ones.

Also, if you found it pleasing, please share this book with the people you love.